MW01148092

Manual on the Art of Living

EPICTETUS

Manual
on the Art
of Living

Translated by
P.E. Matheson

With an Introduction by
Tristan K. Husby

AIORA

Percy Ewing Matheson (1859-1946) was a classical scholar and historian, honorary fellow of New College, Oxford. A prolific author mainly on Roman History, he is principally known for his classic translations of Epictetus' *Discourses* and *Manual*.

Cover artwork: Panagiotis Stavropoulos
Ink on recycled paper produced by Kyra Stratoudaki.

© Aiora Press 2017

First edition May 2017
Reprinted in May 2022

ISBN: 978-618-5048-70-9

AIORA PRESS
11 Mavromichali st.
Athens 10679 - Greece
tel: +30 210 3839000
www.aiorabooks.com

Contents

Whatever I heard him say I used to write down,
word for word, as best I could,
endeavouring to preserve it as a memorial,
for my own future use,
of his way of thinking
and the frankness of his speech.

Arrian

Introduction

Epictetus knows that you can be good, regardless of who you are and regardless of when or where you live.

The *Manual* contains Epictetus' insights on morality, and the pursuit of a good life. Only once you have focused your attention on what is truly good, will you be able to pursue good. For Epictetus, the sole worthwhile aim of life was to be a good person. Even though many moral thinkers before and since have made similar claims, Epictetus' insistence on the absolute centrality of ethical action is still provocative: Epictetus had been a slave and must have been keenly aware that goodness is no protection from a whip.

Living sometime in the first century CE, Epictetus was a slave in Rome, and his owner, Epaphroditos, a Roman senator. Apparently Epaphroditos had sense enough to recognize intellectual talent and invested in Epictetus' education. But how kind Epaphroditos was is a separate question. In his lectures, Epictetus frequently mentions that one of his legs is lame. Early Christian writers, whether eager to allegorize all aspects of Epictetus' life or simply knowledgeable of the cruelty of slavery, imagined that it was Epaphroditos who had broken Epictetus' leg. This we will never know for sure. But what is sure is that, eventually, Ephaphroditos freed Epictetus. Epictetus later left Rome for the small Greek city of Nicopolis, where he founded a school. There he taught the sons of aristocrats, that is, the sons of men like Epaphroditos.

Epictetus so enchanted his student Arrian with his teachings that Arrian wrote the *Discourses*, a record of Epictetus' lectures. Arrian also compiled this *Manual*, which is a collection of Epictetus' moral lessons in the form of a series of aphorisms.

The longest of these reads like a paragraph while the shortest consists of only a few words. Arrian hoped that readers would reflect on each entry, meditating on the possible applications of Epictetus' ethical wisdom. Arrian believed this *Manual* would allow you, the reader, to train yourself to value that which is important in life.

Epictetus was a Stoic philosopher, meaning that his work built upon the precepts and ideas of Zeno of Citium. In the fourth century BCE, Zeno had moved from Citium, a city on the island of Cyprus, to Athens where he studied philosophy and later taught his own followers. Because they gathered in the agora by the *stoa* (a type of portico), the Athenians called these men Stoics. What little of Zeno's work survives depicts a system of thought in which the call to ethical action is both absolute and the only just purpose of life. Although Stoic thinkers, most notably Chrysippus, expanded the range of Stoic philosophy to include sophisticated accounts of logic and cosmology, ethics always remained central.

Epictetus frames the pursuit of philosophy as fundamental to the project of becoming an ethical person, for Stoic philosophy provides arguments that justify the rejection of 'extraneous goods'. Unsurprisingly, for the Stoics as for many moral thinkers, 'extraneous goods' included wealth and power. As Epictetus puts it, 'It is illogical to reason thus, "I am richer than you, therefore I am superior to you".' (44) What is surprising, however, is that the Stoics even included health as an extraneous good. That is, although health is enjoyable, for the Stoics it is not necessary to lead a good life. Instead, they insisted that only the cultivation of the mind is essential: if you cultivate your mind to understand fully Stoic philosophy, you will also train yourself to value only the pursuit of that which is good.

Today the work of Epictetus, and much of Stoicism, has fallen out of style. From the long viewpoint of history, this neglect is new. During the centuries that followed the Renaissance, readers frequently turned to the *Manual* of Epictetus for help

in determining what is important. Indeed, it is because of the work of Stoics like Epictetus, as well as
Seneca and Marcus Aurelius, and their familiarity
to readers in English, that we have derived the adjective 'stoic'.

Notably, the English adjective 'stoic' is not an entirely positive adjective: to be stoic is to be aloof and
withdrawn. And, indeed, much of Epictetus' philosophy requires us to withdraw, both from ourselves
and from other people. Consider his advice on
preparing for death:

> If you kiss your child or your wife, say to yourself
> that you are kissing a human being, for then if
> death strikes it you will not be disturbed. (3)

Epictetus places great value on self-control, and
so he rejects the idea that emotion may have any
worth in deciding whether an action or a goal is
worthy. Such total rejection raises the question of
how many would *want to*, let alone *try to*, follow
Epictetus' philosophy.

The philosophy Epictetus developed was the result of years of studying ancient texts and debating learned men, but it was also knowledge that came as the result of years of self-reflection, self-questioning and the pursuit of survival as a slave. His hard-earned wisdom is apparent in how quickly Epictetus conveys complex ethical ideas in the *Manual*. In Nicopolis, Epictetus was a master teacher, but likely few of his students took up his austere lifestyle in practice; students such as Arrian were the exception, not the rule. Today, some readers may attempt to go in the direction Epictetus points, but many others will respect his passion for goodness and find authenticity in his yearning for it.

Tristan K. Husby

Manual
on the Art
of Living

1

Τῶν ὄντων τὰ μέν ἐστιν ἐφ᾽ ἡμῖν, τὰ δὲ οὐκ ἐφ᾽
ἡμῖν. ἐφ᾽ ἡμῖν μὲν ὑπόληψις, ὁρμή, ὄρεξις, ἔκκλι-
σις καὶ ἑνὶ λόγῳ ὅσα ἡμέτερα ἔργα· οὐκ ἐφ᾽ ἡμῖν
δὲ τὸ σῶμα, ἡ κτῆσις, δόξαι, ἀρχαὶ καὶ ἑνὶ λόγῳ
ὅσα οὐχ ἡμέτερα ἔργα. Καὶ τὰ μὲν ἐφ᾽ ἡμῖν ἐστι
φύσει ἐλεύθερα, ἀκώλυτα, ἀπαραπόδιστα, τὰ δὲ
οὐκ ἐφ᾽ ἡμῖν ἀσθενῆ, δοῦλα, κωλυτά, ἀλλότρια.
Μέμνησο οὖν, ὅτι, ἐὰν τὰ φύσει δοῦλα ἐλεύθερα
οἰηθῇς καὶ τὰ ἀλλότρια ἴδια, ἐμποδισθήσῃ, πεν-
θήσεις, ταραχθήσῃ, μέμψῃ καὶ θεοὺς καὶ ἀνθρώπους, ἐὰν δὲ τὸ σὸν μόνον οἰηθῇς σὸν εἶναι, τὸ δὲ
ἀλλότριον, ὥσπερ ἐστίν, ἀλλότριον, οὐδείς σε
ἀναγκάσει οὐδέποτε, οὐδείς σε κωλύσει, οὐ μέμψῃ οὐδένα, οὐκ ἐγκαλέσεις τινί, ἄκων πράξεις

1

Of all existing things some are in our power, and others are not in our power. In our power are thought, impulse, will to get and will to avoid, and, in a word, everything which is our own doing. Things not in our power include the body, property, reputation, office, and, in a word, everything which is not our own doing. Things in our power are by nature free, unhindered, untrammelled; things not in our power are weak, servile, subject to hindrance, dependent on others. Remember then that if you imagine that what is naturally slavish is free, and what is naturally another's is your own, you will be hampered, you will mourn, you will be put to confusion, you will blame gods and men; but if you think that only your own belongs to you, and that what is another's is indeed another's, no one will ever put

οὐδὲ ἕν, οὐδείς σε βλάψει, ἐχθρὸν οὐχ ἕξεις, οὐδὲ
γὰρ βλαβερόν τι πείσῃ. Τηλικούτων οὖν ἐφιέμε-
νος μέμνησο, ὅτι οὐ δεῖ μετρίως κεκινημένον
ἅπτεσθαι αὐτῶν, ἀλλὰ τὰ μὲν ἀφιέναι παντελῶς,
τὰ δ᾽ ὑπερτίθεσθαι πρὸς τὸ παρόν. ἐὰν δὲ καὶ
ταῦτ᾽ ἐθέλῃς καὶ ἄρχειν καὶ πλουτεῖν, τυχὸν μὲν
οὐδ᾽ αὐτῶν τούτων τεύξῃ διὰ τὸ καὶ τῶν προτέ-
ρων ἐφίεσθαι, πάντως γε μὴν ἐκείνων ἀποτεύξῃ,
δι᾽ ὧν μόνων ἐλευθερία καὶ εὐδαιμονία περιγίνεται. Εὐθὺς οὖν πάσῃ φαντασίᾳ τραχείᾳ μελέτα
ἐπιλέγειν ὅτι «φαντασία εἶ καὶ οὐ πάντως τὸ φαινόμενον».

Ἔπειτα ἐξέταζε αὐτὴν καὶ δοκίμαζε τοῖς κα-
νόσι τούτοις οἷς ἔχεις, πρώτῳ δὲ τούτῳ καὶ μάλιστα, πότερον περὶ τὰ ἐφ᾽ ἡμῖν ἐστιν ἢ περὶ τὰ οὐκ
ἐφ᾽ ἡμῖν· κἂν περί τι τῶν οὐκ ἐφ᾽ ἡμῖν ᾖ, πρόχειρον ἔστω τὸ διότι «οὐδὲν πρὸς ἐμέ».

compulsion or hindrance on you, you will blame none, you will accuse none, you will do nothing against your will, no one will harm you, you will have no enemy, for no harm can touch you.

Aiming then at these high matters, you must remember that to attain them requires more than ordinary effort; you will have to give up some things entirely, and put off others for the moment. And if you would have these also—office and wealth—it may be that you will fail to get them, just because your desire is set on the former, and you will certainly fail to attain those things which alone bring freedom and happiness.

Make it your study then to confront every harsh impression with the words, 'You are but an impression, and not at all what you seem to be.' Then test it by those rules that you possess; and first by this—the chief test of all—'Is it concerned with what is in our power or with what is not in our power?' And if it is concerned with what is not in our power, be ready with the answer that it is nothing to you.

2

Μέμνησο, ὅτι ὀρέξεως ἐπαγγελία ἐπιτυχία, οὗ ὀρέγῃ, ἐκκλίσεως ἐπαγγελία τὸ μὴ περιπεσεῖν ἐκείνῳ, ὃ ἐκκλίνεται, καὶ ὁ μὲν <ἐν> ὀρέξει ἀποτυγχάνων ἀτυχής, ὁ δὲ <ἐν> ἐκκλίσει περιπίπτων δυστυχής. ἂν μὲν οὖν μόνα ἐκκλίνῃς τὰ παρὰ φύσιν τῶν ἐπὶ σοί, οὐδενί, ὧν ἐκκλίνεις, περιπεσῇ· νόσον δ' ἂν ἐκκλίνῃς ἢ θάνατον ἢ πενίαν, δυστυχήσεις.

ἆρον οὖν τὴν ἔκκλισιν ἀπὸ πάντων τῶν οὐκ ἐφ' ἡμῖν καὶ μετάθες ἐπὶ τὰ παρὰ φύσιν τῶν ἐφ' ἡμῖν. τὴν ὄρεξιν δὲ παντελῶς ἐπὶ τοῦ παρόντος ἄνελε· ἄν τε γὰρ ὀρέγῃ τῶν οὐκ ἐφ' ἡμῖν τινος, ἀτυχεῖν ἀνάγκη τῶν τε ἐφ' ἡμῖν, ὅσων ὀρέγεσθαι καλὸν ἄν, οὐδὲν οὐδέπω σοι πάρεστι. μόνῳ δὲ τῷ ὁρμᾶν καὶ ἀφορμᾶν χρῶ, κούφως μέντοι καὶ μεθ' ὑπεξαιρέσεως καὶ ἀνειμένως.

2

Remember that the will to get promises attainment of what you will, and the will to avoid promises escape from what you avoid; and he who fails to get what he wills is unfortunate, and he who does not escape what he wills to avoid is miserable. If then you try to avoid only what is unnatural in the region within your control, you will escape from all that you avoid; but if you try to avoid disease or death or poverty you will be miserable.

Therefore let your will to avoid have no concern with what is not in man's power; direct it only to things in man's power that are contrary to nature. But for the moment you must utterly remove the will to get; for if you will to get something not in man's power you are bound to be unfortunate; while none of the things in man's power that you could honourably will to get is yet within your reach. Impulse to act and not to act, these are your concern; yet exercise them gently and without strain, and provisionally.

3

Ἐφ᾽ ἑκάστου τῶν ψυχαγωγούντων ἢ χρείαν παρε-
χόντων ἢ στεργομένων μέμνησο ἐπιλέγειν, ὁ-
ποῖόν ἐστιν, ἀπὸ τῶν σμικροτάτων ἀρξάμενος· ἂν
χύτραν στέργῃς, ὅτι «χύτραν στέργω». κατεαγεί-
σης γὰρ αὐτῆς οὐ ταραχθήσῃ· ἂν παιδίον σαυτοῦ
καταφιλῇς ἢ γυναῖκα, ὅτι ἄνθρωπον καταφιλεῖς·
ἀποθανόντος γὰρ οὐ ταραχθήσῃ.

4

Ὅταν ἅπτεσθαί τινος ἔργου μέλλῃς, ὑπομίμνησκε
σεαυτόν, ὁποῖόν ἐστι τὸ ἔργον. ἐὰν λουσόμενος
ἀπίῃς, πρόβαλλε σεαυτῷ τὰ γινόμενα ἐν βαλα-
νείῳ, τοὺς ἀπορραίνοντας, τοὺς ἐγκρουομένους,
τοὺς λοιδοροῦντας, τοὺς κλέπτοντας. καὶ οὕτως
ἀσφαλέστερον ἅψῃ τοῦ ἔργου, ἐὰν ἐπιλέγῃς
εὐθὺς ὅτι «λούσασθαι θέλω καὶ τὴν ἐμαυτοῦ
προαίρεσιν κατὰ φύσιν ἔχουσαν τηρῆσαι». καὶ
ὡσαύτως ἐφ᾽ ἑκάστου ἔργου. οὕτω γὰρ ἄν τι

3

When anything, from the meanest thing upwards, is attractive or serviceable or an object of
affection, remember always to say to yourself,
'What is its nature?' If you are fond of a jug, say
you are fond of a jug; then you will not be disturbed if it be broken. If you kiss your child or
your wife, say to yourself that you are kissing a
human being, for then if death strikes it you will
not be disturbed.

4

When you are about to take something in hand,
remind yourself what manner of thing it is. If you
are going to bathe put before your mind what
happens in the bath—water pouring over some,
others being jostled, some reviling, others steal-
ing; and you will set to work more securely if you
say to yourself at once: 'I want to bathe, and I
want to keep my will in harmony with nature,'
and so in each thing you do; for in this way, if
anything turns up to hinder you in your bathing,

πρὸς τὸ λούσασθαι γένηται ἐμποδών, πρόχειρον
ἔσται διότι «ἀλλ' οὐ τοῦτο ἤθελον μόνον, ἀλλὰ
καὶ τὴν ἐμαυτοῦ προαίρεσιν κατὰ φύσιν ἔχουσαν
τηρῆσαι· οὐ τηρήσω δέ, ἐὰν ἀγανακτῶ πρὸς τὰ
γινόμενα».

5

Ταράσσει τοὺς ἀνθρώπους οὐ τὰ πράγματα, ἀλλὰ
τὰ περὶ τῶν πραγμάτων δόγματα· οἷον ὁ θάνατος
οὐδὲν δεινόν (ἐπεὶ καὶ Σωκράτει ἂν ἐφαίνετο),
ἀλλὰ τὸ δόγμα τὸ περὶ τοῦ θανάτου, διότι δεινόν,
ἐκεῖνο τὸ δεινόν ἐστιν. ὅταν οὖν ἐμποδιζώμεθα ἢ
ταρασσώμεθα ἢ λυπώμεθα, μηδέποτε ἄλλον
αἰτιώμεθα, ἀλλ' ἑαυτούς, τοῦτ' ἔστι τὰ ἑαυτῶν
δόγματα. ἀπαιδεύτου ἔργον τὸ ἄλλοις ἐγκαλεῖν,
ἐφ' οἷς αὐτὸς πράσσει κακῶς· ἠργμένου παιδεύε-
σθαι τὸ ἑαυτῷ· πεπαιδευμένου τὸ μήτε ἄλλῳ
μήτε ἑαυτῷ.

you will be ready to say, 'I did not want only to bathe, but to keep my will in harmony with nature, and I shall not so keep it, if I lose my temper at what happens.'

5

What disturbs men's minds is not events but their judgements on events: For instance, death is nothing dreadful, or else Socrates would have thought it so. No, the only dreadful thing about it is men's judgement that it is dreadful. And so when we are hindered, or disturbed, or distressed, let us never lay the blame on others, but on ourselves, that is, on our own judgements. To accuse others for one's own misfortunes is a sign of want of education; to accuse oneself shows that one's education has begun; to accuse neither oneself nor others shows that one's education is complete.

6

Ἐπὶ μηδενὶ ἐπαρθῇς ἀλλοτρίῳ προτερήματι. εἰ ὁ
ἵππος ἐπαιρόμενος ἔλεγεν ὅτι «καλός εἰμι», οἰ-
στὸν ἂν ἦν· σὺ δέ, ὅταν λέγῃς ἐπαιρόμενος ὅτι
«ἵππον καλὸν ἔχω», ἴσθι, ὅτι ἐπὶ ἵππου ἀγαθῷ
ἐπαίρῃ· τί οὖν ἐστι σόν; χρῆσις φαντασιῶν. ὥσθ᾽,
ὅταν ἐν χρήσει φαντασιῶν κατὰ φύσιν σχῇς, τη-
νικαῦτα ἐπάρθητι· τότε γὰρ ἐπὶ σῷ τινι ἀγαθῷ
ἐπαρθήσῃ.

7

Καθάπερ ἐν πλῷ τοῦ πλοίου καθορμισθέντος εἰ
ἐξέλθοις ὑθρεύσασθαι, ὁδοῦ μὲν πάρεργον καὶ
κοχλίδιον ἀναλέξῃ καὶ βολβάριον, τετάσθαι δὲ
δεῖ τὴν διάνοιαν ἐπὶ τὸ πλοῖον καὶ συνεχῶς ἐπι-
στρέφεσθαι, μή ποτε ὁ κυβερνήτης καλέσῃ, κἂν
καλέσῃ, πάντα ἐκεῖνα ἀφιέναι, ἵνα μὴ δεδεμένος
ἐμβληθῇς ὡς τὰ πρόβατα· οὕτω καὶ ἐν τῷ βίῳ,
ἐὰν διδῶται ἀντὶ βολβαρίου καὶ κοχλιδίου γυναι-

6

Be not elated at an excellence which is not your own. If the horse in his pride were to say, 'I am handsome', we could bear with it. But when you say with pride, 'I have a handsome horse', know that the good horse is the ground of your pride. You ask then what you can call your own. The answer is—the way you deal with your impressions. Therefore when you deal with your impressions in accord with nature, then you may be proud indeed, for your pride will be in a good which is your own.

7

When you are on a voyage, and your ship is at anchorage, and you disembark to get fresh water, you may pick up a small shellfish or a truffle by the way, but you must keep your attention fixed on the ship, and keep looking towards it constantly, to see if the Helmsman calls you; and if he does, you have to leave everything, or be bundled on board with your legs tied like a sheep. So

κάριον καὶ παιδίον, οὐδὲν κωλύσει· ἐὰν δὲ ὁ κυβερνήτης καλέσῃ, τρέχε ἐπὶ τὸ πλοῖον ἀφεὶς ἐκεῖνα ἅπαντα μηδὲ ἐπιστρεφόμενος. ἐὰν δὲ γέρων
ᾖς, μηδὲ ἀπαλλαγῇς ποτε τοῦ πλοίου μακράν, μή
ποτε καλοῦντος ἐλλίπῃς.

8

Μὴ ζήτει τὰ γινόμενα γίνεσθαι ὡς θέλεις, ἀλλὰ
θέλε τὰ γινόμενα ὡς γίνεται καὶ εὐροήσεις.

9

Νόσος σώματός ἐστιν ἐμπόδιον, προαιρέσεως δὲ
οὔ, ἐὰν μὴ αὐτὴ θέλῃ. χώλανσις σκέλους ἐστὶν
ἐμπόδιον, προαιρέσεως δὲ οὔ. καὶ τοῦτο ἐφ᾽ ἑκάστου τῶν ἐμπιπτόντων ἐπίλεγε· εὑρήσεις γὰρ
αὐτὸ ἄλλου τινὸς ἐμπόδιον, σὸν δὲ οὔ.

it is in life. If you have a dear wife or child given you, they are like the shellfish or the truffle, they are very well in their way. Only, if the Helmsman call, run back to your ship, leave all else, and do not look behind you. And if you are old, never go far from the ship, so that when you are called you may not fail to appear.

8

Ask not that events should happen as you will, but let your will be that events should happen as they do, and you shall have peace.

9

Sickness is a hindrance to the body, but not to the will, unless the will consent. Lameness is a hindrance to the leg, but not to the will. Say this to yourself at each event that happens, for you shall find that though it hinders something else it will not hinder you.

10

Ἐφ᾽ ἑκάστου τῶν προσπιπτόντων μέμνησο ἐπι-
στρέφων ἐπὶ σεαυτὸν ζητεῖν, τίνα δύναμιν ἔχεις
πρὸς τὴν χρῆσιν αὐτοῦ. ἐὰν καλὸν ἴδῃς ἢ καλήν,
εὑρήσεις δύναμιν πρὸς ταῦτα ἐγκράτειαν· ἐὰν
πόνος προσφέρηται, εὑρήσεις καρτερίαν· ἂν λοι-
δορία, εὑρήσεις ἀνεξικακίαν. καὶ οὕτως ἐθιζόμε-
νόν σε οὐ συναρπάσουσιν αἱ φαντασίαι.

11

Μηδέποτε ἐπὶ μηδενὸς εἴπῃς ὅτι «ἀπώλεσα
αὐτό», ἀλλ᾽ ὅτι «ἀπέδωκα». τὸ παιδίον ἀπέθανεν;
ἀπεδόθη. ἡ γυνὴ ἀπέθανεν; ἀπεδόθη. «τὸ χωρίον
ἀφῃρέθην». οὐκοῦν καὶ τοῦτο ἀπεδόθη. «ἀλλὰ
κακὸς ὁ ἀφελόμενος». τί δὲ σοὶ μέλει, διὰ τίνος
σε ὁ δοὺς ἀπήτησε; μέχρι δ᾽ ἂν διδῷ, ὡς ἀλλο-
τρίου αὐτοῦ ἐπιμελοῦ, ὡς τοῦ πανδοχείου οἱ πα-
ριόντες.

10

When anything happens to you, always remember to turn to yourself and ask what faculty you have to deal with it. If you see a beautiful boy or a beautiful woman, you will find continence the faculty to exercise there; if trouble is laid on you, you will find endurance; if ribaldry, you will find patience. And if you train yourself in this habit your impressions will not carry you away.

11

Never say of anything, 'I lost it', but say, 'I gave it back'. Has your child died? It was given back. Has your wife died? She was given back. Has your estate been taken from you? Was not this also given back? But you say, 'He who took it from me is wicked'. What does it matter to you through whom the Giver asked it back? As long as He gives it you, take care of it, but not as your own; treat it as passers-by treat an inn.

12

Εἰ προκόψαι θέλεις, ἄφες τοὺς τοιούτους ἐπιλο-
γισμούς. «ἐὰν ἀμελήσω τᾶν ἐμῶν, οὐχ ἕξω δια-
τροφάς»· «ἐὰν μὴ κολάσω τὸν παῖδα, πονηρὸς
ἔσται». κρεῖσσον γὰρ λιμῷ ἀποθανεῖν ἄλυπον καὶ
ἄφοβον γενόμενον ἢ ζῆν ἐν ἀφθόνοις ταρασσό-
μενον. κρεῖττον δὲ τὸν παῖδα κακὸν εἶναι ἢ σὲ κα-
κοδαίμονα. ἄρξαι τοιγαροῦν ἀπὸ τῶν σμικρῶν.
ἐκχεῖται τὸ ἐλάδιον, κλέπτεται τὸ οἰνάριον· ἐπί-
λεγε ὅτι «τοσούτου πωλεῖται ἀπάθεια, τοσούτου
ἀταραξία»· προῖκα δὲ οὐδὲν περιγίνεται. ὅταν δὲ
καλῇς τὸν παῖδα, ἐνθυμοῦ, ὅτι δύναται μὴ ὑπα-
κοῦσαι καὶ ὑπακούσας μηδὲν ποιῆσαι ὧν θέλεις·
ἀλλ᾿ οὐχ οὕτως ἐστὶν αὐτῷ καλῶς, ἵνα ἐπ᾿ ἐκείνῳ
ᾖ τὸ σὲ μὴ ταραχθῆναι.

12

If you wish to make progress, abandon reasonings of this sort: 'If I neglect my affairs I shall have nothing to live on'; 'If I do not punish my son, he will be wicked.' For it is better to die of hunger, so that you be free from pain and free from fear, than to live in plenty and be troubled in mind. It is better for your son to be wicked than for you to be miserable. Wherefore begin with little things. Is your drop of oil spilt? Is your sup of wine stolen? Say to yourself, 'This is the price paid for freedom from passion, this is the price of a quiet mind.' Nothing can be had without a price. When you call your slave-boy, reflect that he may not be able to hear you, and if he hears you, he may not be able to do anything you want. But he is not so well off that it rests with him to give you peace of mind.

13

Εἰ προκόψαι θέλεις, ὑπόμεινον ἕνεκα τῶν ἐκτὸς
ἀνόητος δόξας καὶ ἠλίθιος, μηδὲν βούλου δοκεῖν
ἐπίστασθαι· κἂν δόξῃς τις εἶναί τισιν, ἀπίστει σεαυτῷ. ἴσθι γὰρ ὅτι οὐ ῥᾴδιον τὴν προαίρεσιν τὴν
σεαυτοῦ κατὰ φύσιν ἔχουσαν φυλάξαι καὶ τὰ
ἐκτός, ἀλλὰ τοῦ ἑτέρου ἐπιμελούμενον τοῦ ἑτέρου ἀμελῆσαι πᾶσα ἀνάγκη.

14

Ἐὰν θέλῃς τὰ τέκνα σου καὶ τὴν γυναῖκα καὶ
τοὺς φίλους σου πάντοτε ζῆν, ἠλίθιος εἶ· τὰ γὰρ
μὴ ἐπὶ σοὶ θέλεις ἐπὶ σοὶ εἶναι καὶ τὰ ἀλλότρια σὰ
εἶναι. οὕτω κἂν τὸν παῖδα θέλῃς μὴ ἁμαρτάνειν,
μωρὸς εἶ· θέλεις γὰρ τὴν κακίαν μὴ εἶναι κακίαν,
ἀλλ᾽ ἄλλο τι. ἐὰν δὲ θέλῃς ὀρεγόμενος μὴ ἀπο-
τυγχάνειν, τοῦτο δύνασαι. τοῦτο οὖν ἄσκει, ὃ
δύνασαι.

κύριος ἑκάστου ἐστὶν ὁ τῶν ὑπ᾽ ἐκείνου θελο-

13

If you wish to make progress, you must be content in external matters to seem a fool and a simpleton; do not wish men to think you know anything, and if any should think you to be somebody, distrust yourself. For know that it is not easy to keep your will in accord with nature and at the same time keep outward things; if you attend to one you must needs neglect the other.

14

It is silly to want your children and your wife and your friends to live forever, for that means that you want what is not in your control to be in your control, and what is not your own to be yours. In the same way if you want your servant to make no mistakes, you are a fool, for you want vice not to be vice but something different. But if you want not to be disappointed in your will to get, you can attain to that.

Exercise yourself then in what lies in your power. Each man's master is the man who has au-

μένων ἢ μὴ θελομένων ἔχων τὴν ἐξουσίαν εἰς τὸ
περιποιῆσαι ἢ ἀφελέσθαι. ὅστις οὖν ἐλεύθερος
εἶναι βούλεται, μήτε θελέτω τι μήτε φευγέτω τι
τῶν ἐπ᾽ ἄλλοις· εἰ δὲ μή, δουλεύειν ἀνάγκη.

15

Μέμνησο, ὅτι ὡς ἐν συμποσίῳ σε δεῖ ἀναστρέφε-
σθαι. περιφερόμενον γέγονέ τι κατὰ σέ· ἐκτείνας
τὴν χεῖρα κοσμίως μετάλαβε. παρέρχεται· μὴ κά-
τεχε. οὔπω ἥκει· μὴ ἐπίβαλλε πόρρω τὴν ὄρεξιν,
ἀλλὰ περίμενε, μέχρις ἂν γένηται κατὰ σέ. οὕτω
πρὸς τέκνα, οὕτω πρὸς γυναῖκα, οὕτω πρὸς
ἀρχάς, οὕτω πρὸς πλοῦτον· καὶ ἔσῃ ποτὲ ἄξιος
τῶν θεῶν συμπότης. ἂν δὲ καὶ παρατεθέντων σοι
μὴ λάβῃς, ἀλλ᾽ ὑπερίδῃς, τότε οὐ μόνον συμπότης τῶν θεῶν ἔσῃ, ἀλλὰ καὶ συνάρχων. οὕτω γὰρ
ποιῶν Διογένης καὶ Ἡράκλειτος καὶ οἱ ὅμοιοι
ἀξίως θεῖοί τε ἦσαν καὶ ἐλέγοντο.

MANUAL ON THE ART OF LIVING

thority over what he wishes or does not wish, to
secure the one or to take away the other. Let him
then who wishes to be free not wish for anything
or avoid anything that depends on others; or else
he is bound to be a slave.

15

Remember that you must behave in life as you
would at a banquet. A dish is handed round and
comes to you; put out your hand and take it po-
litely. It passes you; do not stop it. It has not
reached you; do not be impatient to get it, but
wait till your turn comes. Bear yourself thus towards children, wife, office, wealth, and one day
you will be worthy to banquet with the gods. But
if when they are set before you, you do not take
them but despise them, then you shall not only
share the gods' banquet, but shall share their rule.
For by so doing Diogenes and Heraclitus and
men like them were called divine and deserved
the name.

16

Ὅταν κλαίοντα ἴδῃς τινὰ ἐν πένθει ἢ ἀποδη-
μοῦντος τέκνου ἢ ἀπολωλεκότα τὰ ἑαυτοῦ, πρόσεχε μή σε ἡ φαντασία συναρπάσῃ ὡς ἐν κακοῖς
ὄντος αὐτοῦ τοῖς ἐκτός, ἀλλ᾽ εὐθὺς ἔστω πρόχειρον ὅτι «τοῦτον θλίβει οὐ τὸ συμβεβηκός (ἄλλον
γὰρ οὐ θλίβει), ἀλλὰ τὸ δόγμα τὸ περὶ τούτου».
μέχρι μέντοι λόγου μὴ ὄκνει συμπεριφέρεσθαι
αὐτῷ, κἂν οὕτω τύχῃ, καὶ συνεπιστενάξαι· πρόσεχε μέντοι μὴ καὶ ἔσωθεν στενάξῃς.

17

Μέμνησο, ὅτι ὑποκριτὴς εἶ δράματος, οἵου ἂν
θέλῃ ὁ διδάσκαλος· ἂν βραχύ, βραχέος· ἂν μα-
κρόν, μακροῦ· ἂν πτωχὸν ὑποκρίνασθαί σε θέλῃ,
ἵνα καὶ τοῦτον εὐφυῶς ὑποκρίνῃ ἂν χωλόν, ἂν
ἄρχοντα, ἂν ἰδιώτην. σὸν γὰρ τοῦτ᾽ ἔστι, τὸ δο-
θὲν ὑποκρίνασθαι πρόσωπον καλῶς· ἐκλέξασθαι
δ᾽ αὐτὸ ἄλλου.

16

When you see a man shedding tears in sorrow for a child abroad or dead, or for loss of property, beware that you are not carried away by the impression that it is outward ills that make him miserable. Keep this thought by you: 'What distresses him is not the event, for that does not distress another, but his judgement on the event.' Therefore do not hesitate to sympathize with him so far as words go, and if it so chance, even to groan with him; but take heed that you do not also groan in your inner being.

17

Remember that you are an actor in a play, and the Playwright chooses the manner of it: if he wants it short, it is short; if long, it is long. If he wants you to act a poor man you must act the part with all your powers; and so if your part be a cripple or a magistrate or a plain man. For your business is to act the character that is given you and act it well; the choice of the cast is Another's.

18

Κόραξ ὅταν μὴ αἴσιον κεκράγῃ, μὴ συναρπαζέτω
σε ἡ φαντασία· ἀλλ᾿ εὐθὺς διαίρει παρὰ σεαυτῷ
καὶ λέγε ὅτι «τούτων ἐμοὶ οὐδὲν ἐπισημαίνεται,
ἀλλ᾿ ἢ τῷ σωματίῳ μου ἢ τῷ κτησειδίῳ μου ἢ τῷ
δοξαρίῳ μου ἢ τοῖς τέκνοις ἢ τῇ γυναικί. ἐμοὶ δὲ
πάντα αἴσια σημαίνεται, ἐὰν ἐγὼ θέλω· ὅ τι γὰρ
ἂν τούτων ἀποβαίνῃ, ἐπ᾿ ἐμοί ἐστιν ὠφεληθῆναι
ἀπ᾿ αὐτοῦ».

19

Ἀνίκητος εἶναι δύνασαι, ἐὰν εἰς μηδένα ἀγῶνα
καταβαίνῃς, ὃν οὐκ ἔστιν ἐπὶ σοὶ νικῆσαι. ὅρα μήποτε ἰδών τινα προτιμώμενον ἢ μέγα δυνάμενον
ἢ ἄλλως εὐδοκιμοῦντα μακαρίσῃς, ὑπὸ τῆς φαντασίας συναρπασθείς. ἐὰν γὰρ ἐν τοῖς ἐφ᾿ ἡμῖν ἡ
οὐσία τοῦ ἀγαθοῦ ᾖ, οὔτε φθόνος οὔτε ζηλοτυπία
χώραν ἔχει· σύ τε αὐτὸς οὐ στρατηγός, οὐ πρύτα-
νις ἢ ὕπατος εἶναι θελήσεις, ἀλλ᾿ ἐλεύθερος. μία

18

When a raven croaks with evil omen, let not the impression carry you away, but straightway distinguish in your own mind and say, 'These portents mean nothing to me; but only to my bit of a body or my bit of property or name, or my children or my wife. But for me all omens are favourable if I will, for, whatever the issue may be, it is in my power to put benefit therefrom.'

19

You can be invincible, if you never enter on a contest where victory is not in your power. Beware then that when you see a man raised to honour or great power or high repute you do not let your impression carry you away. For if the reality of good lies in what is in our power, there is no room for envy or jealousy. And you will not wish to be praetor, or prefect or consul, but to be free; and there is but one way to freedom—to despise what is not in our power.

δὲ ὁδὸς πρὸς τοῦτο, καταφρόνησις τῶν οὐκ ἐφ᾽
ἡμῖν.

20

Μέμνησο, ὅτι οὐχ ὁ λοιδορῶν ἢ ὁ τύπτων ὑβρί-
ζει, ἀλλὰ τὸ δόγμα τὸ περὶ τούτων ὡς ὑβριζό-
ντων. ὅταν οὖν ἐρεθίσῃ σέ τις, ἴσθι, ὅτι ἡ σή σε
ὑπόληψις ἠρέθικε. τοιγαροῦν ἐν πρώτοις πειρῶ
ὑπὸ τῆς φαντασίας μὴ συναρπασθῆναι· ἂν γὰρ
ἅπαξ χρόνου καὶ διατριβῆς τύχῃς, ῥᾷον κρατή-
σεις σεαυτοῦ.

21

Θάνατος καὶ φυγὴ καὶ πάντα τὰ δεινὰ φαινόμενα
πρὸ ὀφθαλμῶν ἔστω σοι καθ᾽ ἡμέραν, μάλιστα δὲ
πάντων ὁ θάνατος· καὶ οὐδὲν οὐδέποτε οὔτε τα-
πεινὸν ἐνθυμηθήσῃ οὔτε ἄγαν ἐπιθυμήσεις τινός.

20

Remember that foul words or blows in themselves are no outrage, but your judgement that they are so. So when anyone makes you angry, know that it is your own thought that has angered you. Wherefore make it your first endeavour not to let your impressions carry you away. For if once you gain time and delay, you will find it easier to control yourself.

21

Keep before your eyes from day to day death and exile and all things that seem terrible, but death most of all, and then you will never set your thoughts on what is low and will never desire anything beyond measure.

22

Εἰ φιλοσοφίας ἐπιθυμεῖς, παρασκευάζου αὐτόθεν ὡς καταγελασθησόμενος, ὡς καταμωκησομένων σου πολλῶν, ὡς ἐρούντων ὅτι «ἄφνω φιλόσοφος ἡμῖν ἐπανελήλυθε» καὶ «πόθεν ἡμῖν αὕτη ἡ ὀφρύς;» σὺ δὲ ὀφρὺν μὲν μὴ σχῇς· τῶν δὲ βελτίστων σοι φαινομένων οὕτως ἔχου, ὡς ὑπὸ τοῦ θεοῦ τεταγμένος εἰς ταύτην τὴν χώραν· μέμνησό τε διότι, ἐὰν μὲν ἐμμείνῃς τοῖς αὐτοῖς, οἱ καταγελῶντές σου τὸ πρότερον οὗτοί σε ὕστερον θαυμάσονται, ἐὰν δὲ ἡττηθῇς αὐτῶν, διπλοῦν προσλήψῃ καταγέλωτα.

23

Ἐάν ποτέ σοι γένηται ἔξω στραφῆναι πρὸς τὸ βούλεσθαι ἀρέσαι τινί, ἴσθι ὅτι ἀπώλεσας τὴν ἔνστασιν. ἀρκοῦ οὖν ἐν παντὶ τῷ εἶναι φιλόσοφος· εἰ δὲ καὶ δοκεῖν βούλει [τῷ εἶναι], σαυτῷ φαίνου καὶ ἱκανὸς ἔσῃ.

22

If you set your desire on philosophy you must at once prepare to meet with ridicule and the jeers of many who will say, 'Here he is again, turned philosopher. Where has he got these proud looks?' Nay, put on no proud looks, but hold fast to what seems best to you, in confidence that God has set you at this post. And remember that if you abide where you are, those who first laugh at you will one day admire you, and that if you give way to them, you will get doubly laughed at.

23

If it ever happen to you to be diverted to things outside, so that you desire to please another, know that you have lost your life's plan. Be content then always to be a philosopher; if you wish to be regarded as one too, show yourself that you are one and you will be able to achieve it.

24

Οὗτοί σε οἱ διαλογισμοὶ μὴ θλιβέτωσαν «ἄτιμος ἐγὼ βιώσομαι καὶ οὐδεὶς οὐδαμοῦ». εἰ γὰρ ἡ ἀτιμία ἐστὶ κακόν, οὐ δύνασαι ἐν κακῷ εἶναι δι᾽ ἄλλον, οὐ μᾶλλον ἢ ἐν αἰσχρῷ· μή τι οὖν σόν ἐστιν ἔργον τὸ ἀρχῆς τυχεῖν ἢ παραληφθῆναι ἐφ᾽ ἑστίασιν;

οὐδαμῶς.

πῶς οὖν ἔτι τοῦτ᾽ ἔστιν ἀτιμία; πῶς δὲ οὐδεὶς οὐδαμοῦ ἔσῃ, ὃν ἐν μόνοις εἶναί τινα δεῖ τοῖς ἐπὶ σοί, ἐν οἷς ἔξεστί σοι εἶναι πλείστου ἀξίῳ; ἀλλά σοι οἱ φίλοι ἀβοήθητοι ἔσονται.

τί λέγεις τὸ ἀβοήθητοι; οὐχ ἕξουσι παρὰ σοῦ κερμάτιον· οὐδὲ πολίτας Ῥωμαίων αὐτοὺς ποιήσεις. τίς οὖν σοι εἶπεν, ὅτι ταῦτα τῶν ἐφ᾽ ἡμῖν ἐστιν, οὐχὶ δὲ ἀλλότρια ἔργα; τίς δὲ δοῦναι δύναται ἑτέρῳ, ἃ μὴ ἔχει αὐτός;

«κτῆσαι οὖν», φησίν, «ἵνα ἡμεῖς ἔχωμεν».

εἰ δύναμαι κτήσασθαι τηρῶν ἐμαυτὸν αἰδή-

24

Let not reflections such as these afflict you: 'I shall live without honour, and never be of any account'; for if lack of honour is an evil, no one but yourself can involve you in evil any more than in shame. Is it your business to get office or to be invited to an entertainment?

Certainly not.

Where then is the dishonour you talk of? How can you be 'of no account anywhere', when you ought to count for something in those matters only which are in your power, where you may achieve the highest worth? 'But my friends,' you say, 'will lack assistance.'

What do you mean by 'lack assistance'? They will not have cash from you and you will not make them Roman citizens. Who told you that to do these things is in our power, and not dependent upon others? Who can give to another what is not his to give?

'Get them then,' says he, 'that we may have them.'

μονα καὶ πιστὸν καὶ μεγαλόφρονα, δείκνυε τὴν
ὁδὸν καὶ κτήσομαι. εἰ δ᾽ ἐμὲ ἀξιοῦτε τὰ ἀγαθὰ τὰ
ἐμαυτοῦ ἀπολέσαι, ἵνα ὑμεῖς τὰ μὴ ἀγαθὰ περι-
ποιήσησθε, ὁρᾶτε ὑμεῖς, πῶς ἄνισοί ἐστε καὶ ἀ-
γνώμονες. τί δὲ καὶ βούλεσθε μᾶλλον; ἀργύριον
ἢ φίλον πιστὸν καὶ αἰδήμονα; εἰς τοῦτο οὖν μοι
μᾶλλον συλλαμβάνετε καὶ μή, δι᾽ ὧν ἀποβαλῶ
αὐτὰ ταῦτα, ἐκεῖνά με πράσσειν ἀξιοῦτε.

«ἀλλ᾽ ἡ πατρίς, ὅσον ἐπ᾽ ἐμοί», φησίν, «ἀβοή-
θητος ἔσται». πάλιν, ποίαν καὶ ταύτην βοήθειαν;

στοὰς οὐχ ἕξει διὰ σὲ οὔτε βαλανεῖα. καὶ τί
τοῦτο; οὐδὲ γὰρ ὑποδήματα ἔχει διὰ τὸν χαλκέα
οὐδ᾽ ὅπλα διὰ τὸν σκυτέα· ἱκανὸν δέ, ἐὰν ἕκα-
στος ἐκπληρώσῃ τὸ ἑαυτοῦ ἔργον. εἰ δὲ ἄλλον
τινὰ αὐτῇ κατεσκεύαζες πολίτην πιστὸν καὶ αἰδήμονα, οὐδὲν ἂν αὐτὴν ὠφέλεις;

«ναί».

οὐκοῦν οὐδὲ σὺ αὐτὸς ἀνωφελὴς ἂν εἴης αὐτῇ.

«τίνα οὖν ἕξω», φησί, «χώραν ἐν τῇ πόλει;»

If I can get them and keep my self-respect, honour, magnanimity, show the way and I will get them. But if you call on me to lose the good things that are mine, in order that you may win things that are not good, look how unfair and thoughtless you are. And which do you really prefer? Money, or a faithful, modest friend? Therefore help me rather to keep these qualities, and do not expect from me actions which will make me lose them.

'But my country,' says he, 'will lack assistance, so far as lies in me.'

Once more I ask, What assistance do you mean? It will not owe colonnades or baths to you. What of that? It does not owe shoes to the blacksmith or arms to the shoemaker; it is sufficient if each man fulfils his own function. Would you do it no good if you secured to it another faithful and modest citizen?

'Yes.'

Well, then, you would not be useless to it.

'What place then shall I have in the city?'

ἣν ἂν δύνῃ φυλάττων ἅμα τὸν πιστὸν καὶ αἰδήμονα. εἰ δὲ ἐκείνην ὠφελεῖν βουλόμενος ἀπο-
βαλεῖς ταῦτα, τί ὄφελος ἂν αὐτῇ γένοιο ἀναιδὴς
καὶ ἄπιστος ἀποτελεσθείς;

25

Προετιμήθη σού τις ἐν ἑστιάσει ἢ ἐν προσαγο-
ρεύσει ἢ ἐν τῷ παραληφθῆναι εἰς συμβουλίαν; εἰ
μὲν ἀγαθὰ ταῦτά ἐστι, χαίρειν σε δεῖ, ὅτι ἔτυχεν
αὐτῶν ἐκεῖνος· εἰ δὲ κακά, μὴ ἄχθου, ὅτι σὺ
αὐτῶν οὐκ ἔτυχες· μέμνησο δέ, ὅτι οὐ δύνασαι μὴ
ταὐτὰ ποιῶν πρὸς τὸ τυγχάνειν τῶν οὐκ ἐφ᾽ ἡμῖν
τῶν ἴσων ἀξιοῦσθαι. πῶς γὰρ ἴσον ἔχειν δύναται
ὁ μὴ φοιτῶν ἐπὶ θύρας τινὸς τῷ φοιτῶντι; ὁ μὴ
παραπέμπων τῷ παραπέμποντι; ὁ μὴ ἐπαινῶν τῷ
ἐπαινοῦντι, ἄδικος οὖν ἔσῃ καὶ ἄπληστος, εἰ μὴ
προϊέμενος ταῦτα, ἀνθ᾽ ὧν ἐκεῖνα πιπράσκεται,
προῖκα αὐτὰ βουλήσῃ λαμβάνειν. ἀλλὰ πόσου πι-
πράσκονται θρίδακες; ὀβολοῦ, ἂν οὕτω τύχῃ. ἂν

Whatever place you can hold while you keep your character for honour and self-respect. But if you are going to lose these qualities in trying to benefit your city, what benefit, I ask, would you have done her when you attain to the perfection of being lost to shame and honour?

25

Has someone had precedence of you at an entertainment or a levée or been called in before you to give advice? If these things are good you ought to be glad that he got them; if they are evil, do not be angry that you did not get them yourself. Remember that if you want to get what is not in your power, you cannot earn the same reward as others unless you act as they do. How is it possible for one who does not haunt the great man's door to have equal shares with one who does, or one who does not go in his train equality with one who does; or one who does not praise him with one who does? You will be unjust then and insatiable if you wish to get these privileges for

οὖν τις προέμενος τὸν ὀβολὸν λάβῃ θρίδακας, σὺ
δὲ μὴ προέμενος μὴ λάβῃς, μὴ οἴου ἔλαττον ἔχειν
τοῦ λαβόντος. ὡς γὰρ ἐκεῖνος ἔχει θρίδακας,
οὕτω σὺ τὸν ὀβολόν, ὃν οὐκ ἔδωκας. τὸν αὐτὸν
δὴ τρόπον καὶ ἐνταῦθα. οὐ παρεκλήθης ἐφ᾽ ἑστί-
ασίν τινος; οὐ γὰρ ἔδωκας τῷ καλοῦντι, ὅσου
πωλεῖ τὸ δεῖπνον. ἐπαίνου δ᾽ αὐτὸ πωλεῖ, θερα-
πείας πωλεῖ. δὸς οὖν τὸ διάφορον, εἴ σοι λυσι-
τελεῖ, ὅσου πωλεῖται. εἰ δὲ κἀκεῖνα θέλεις μὴ
προΐεσθαι καὶ ταῦτα λαμβάνειν, ἄπληστος εἶ καὶ
ἀβέλτερος.

οὐδὲν οὖν ἔχεις ἀντὶ τοῦ δείπνου;

ἔχεις μὲν οὖν τὸ μὴ ἐπαινέσαι τοῦτον, ὃν οὐκ
ἤθελες, τὸ μὴ ἀνασχέσθαι αὐτοῦ τῶν ἐπὶ τῆς εἰ-
σόδου.

nothing, without paying their price. What is the price of a lettuce? An obol perhaps. If then a man pays his obol and gets his lettuces, and you do not pay and do not get them, do not think you are defrauded. For as he has the lettuces so you have the obol you did not give. The same principle holds good too in conduct. You were not invited to someone's entertainment? Because you did not give the host the price for which he sells his dinner. He sells it for compliments, he sells it for attentions. Pay him the price then, if it is to your profit. But if you wish to get the one and yet not give up the other, nothing can satisfy you in your folly.

What! you say, you have nothing instead of the dinner?

Nay, you have this, you have not praised the man you did not want to praise, you have not had to bear with the insults of his doorstep.

26

Τὸ βούλημα τῆς φύσεως καταμαθεῖν ἔστιν ἐξ
ὧν οὐ διαφερόμεθα πρὸς ἀλλήλους. οἷον, ὅταν
ἄλλου παιδάριον κατεάξῃ τὸ ποτήριον, πρόχειρον εὐθὺς λέγειν ὅτι «τῶν γινομένων ἐστίν». ἴ-
σθι οὖν, ὅτι, ὅταν καὶ τὸ σὸν κατεαγῇ, τοιοῦτον
εἶναί σε δεῖ, ὁποῖον ὅτε καὶ τὸ τοῦ ἄλλου κατε-
άγη. οὕτω μετατίθει καὶ ἐπὶ τὰ μείζονα. τέκνον
ἄλλου τέθνηκεν ἢ γυνή; οὐδείς ἐστιν ὃς οὐκ ἂν
εἴποι ὅτι «ἀνθρώπινον»· ἀλλ᾽ ὅταν τὸ αὑτοῦ
τινος ἀποθάνῃ, εὐθὺς «οἴμοι, τάλας ἐγώ». ἐχρῆν
δὲ μεμνῆσθαι, τί πάσχομεν περὶ ἄλλων αὐτὸ
ἀκούσαντες.

27

Ὥσπερ σκοπὸς πρὸς τὸ ἀποτυχεῖν οὐ τίθεται,
οὕτως οὐδὲ κακοῦ φύσις ἐν κόσμῳ γίνεται.

26

It is in our power to discover the will of Nature from those matters on which we have no difference of opinion. For instance, when another man's slave has broken the wine-cup we are very ready to say at once, 'Such things must happen'. Know then that when your own cup is broken, you ought to behave in the same way as when your neighbour's was broken. Apply the same principle to higher matters. Is another's child or wife dead? Not one of us but would say, 'Such is the lot of man'; but when one's own dies, straightway one cries, 'Alas! miserable am I'. But we ought to remember what our feelings are when we hear it of another.

27

As a mark is not set up for men to miss it, so there is nothing intrinsically evil in the world.

28

Εἰ μὲν τὸ σῶμά σού τις ἐπέτρεπε τῷ ἀπαντήσαντι, ἠγανάκτεις ἄν· ὅτι δὲ σὺ τὴν γνώμην τὴν σεαυτοῦ ἐπιτρέπεις τῷ τυχόντι, ἵνα, ἐὰν λοιδορήσηταί σοι, ταραχθῇ ἐκείνη καὶ συγχυθῇ, οὐκ αἰσχύνῃ τούτου ἕνεκα;

29

Ἑκάστου ἔργου σκόπει τὰ καθηγούμενα καὶ τὰ ἀκόλουθα αὐτοῦ καὶ οὕτως ἔρχου ἐπ᾽ αὐτό. εἰ δὲ μή, τὴν μὲν πρώτην προθύμως ἥξεις ἅτε μηδὲν τῶν ἑξῆς ἐντεθυμημένος, ὕστερον δὲ ἀναφανέντων δυσχερῶν τινων αἰσχρῶς ἀποστήσῃ. θέλεις Ὀλύμπια νικῆσαι; κἀγώ, νὴ τοὺς θεούς· κομψὸν γάρ ἐστιν. ἀλλὰ σκόπει τὰ καθηγούμενα καὶ τὰ ἀκόλουθα καὶ οὕτως ἅπτου τοῦ ἔργου. δεῖ σ᾽ εὐτακτεῖν, ἀναγκοτροφεῖν, ἀπέχεσθαι πεμμάτων, γυμνάζεσθαι πρὸς ἀνάγκην, ἐν ὥρᾳ τεταγμένῃ, ἐν καύματι, ἐν ψύχει, μὴ ψυχρὸν πίνειν, μὴ οἶνον, ὡς

28

If anyone trusted your body to the first man he met, you would be indignant, but yet you trust your mind to the chance corner, and allow it to be disturbed and confounded if he revile you; are you not ashamed to do so?

29

In everything you do consider what comes first and what follows, and so approach it. Otherwise you will come to it with a good heart at first because you have not reflected on any of the consequences, and afterwards, when difficulties have appeared, you will desist to your shame. Do you wish to win at Olympia? So do I, by the gods, for it is a fine thing. But consider the first steps to it, and the consequences, and so lay your hand to the work. You must submit to discipline, eat to order, touch no sweets, train under compulsion, at a fixed hour, in heat and cold, drink no cold water, nor wine, except by order; you must hand yourself over completely to your trainer as you

ἔτυχεν, ἁπλῶς ὡς ἰατρῷ παραδεδωκέναι σεαυτὸν
τῷ ἐπιστάτῃ, εἶτα ἐν τῷ ἀγῶνι παρορύσσεσθαι,
ἔστι δὲ ὅτε χεῖρα ἐκβαλεῖν, σφυρὸν στρέψαι, πολ-
λὴν ἁφὴν καταπιεῖν, ἔσθ' ὅτε μαστιγωθῆναι καὶ
μετὰ τούτων πάντων νικηθῆναι. ταῦτα ἐπισκεψά-
μενος, ἂν ἔτι θέλῃς, ἔρχου ἐπὶ τὸ ἀθλεῖν. εἰ δὲ μή,
ὡς τὰ παιδία ἀναστραφήσῃ, ἃ νῦν μὲν παλαιστὰς
παίζει, νῦν δὲ μονομάχους, νῦν δὲ σαλπίζει, εἶτα
τραγῳδεῖ· οὕτω καὶ σὺ νῦν μὲν ἀθλητής, νῦν δὲ
μονομάχος, εἶτα ῥήτωρ, εἶτα φιλόσοφος, ὅλῃ δὲ τῇ
ψυχῇ οὐδέν· ἀλλ' ὡς πίθηκος πᾶσαν θέαν, ἣν ἂν
ἴδῃς, μιμῇ καὶ ἄλλο ἐξ ἄλλου σοι ἀρέσκει. οὐ γὰρ
μετὰ σκέψεως ἦλθες ἐπί τι οὐδὲ περιοδεύσας, ἀλλ'
εἰκῆ καὶ κατὰ ψυχρὰν ἐπιθυμίαν. οὕτω θεασάμενοί
τινες φιλόσοφον καὶ ἀκούσαντες οὕτω τινὸς λέγον-
τος, ὡς Εὐφράτης λέγει (καίτοι τίς οὕτω δύναται
εἰπεῖν, ὡς ἐκεῖνος;), θέλουσι καὶ αὐτοὶ φιλοσοφεῖν.

ἄνθρωπε, πρῶτον ἐπίσκεψαι, ὁποῖόν ἐστι τὸ
πρᾶγμα· εἶτα καὶ τὴν σεαυτοῦ φύσιν κατάμαθε, εἰ

would to a physician, and then when the contest comes you must risk getting hacked, and sometimes dislocate your hand, twist your ankle, swallow plenty of sand, sometimes get a flogging, and with all this suffer defeat. When you have considered all this well, then enter on the athlete's course, if you still wish it. If you act without thought you will be behaving like children, who one day play at wrestlers, another day at gladiators, now sound the trumpet, and next strut the stage. Like them you will be now an athlete, now a gladiator, then orator, then philosopher, but nothing with all your soul. Like an ape, you imitate every sight you see, and one thing after another takes your fancy. When you undertake a thing you do it casually and halfheartedly, instead of considering it and looking at it all round. In the same way some people, when they see a philosopher and hear a man speaking like Euphrates (and indeed who can speak as he can?), wish to be philosophers themselves.

Man, consider first what it is you are under-

δύνασαι βαστάσαι. πένταθλος εἶναι βούλει ἢ πα-
λαιστής; ἴδε σεαυτοῦ τοὺς βραχίονας, τοὺς μη-
ρούς, τὴν ὀσφὺν κατάμαθε. ἄλλος γὰρ πρὸς ἄλλο
πέφυκε. δοκεῖς, ὅτι ταῦτα ποιῶν ὡσαύτως δύνασαι ἐσθίειν, ὡσαύτως πίνειν, ὁμοίως ὀρέγεσθαι,
ὁμοίως δυσαρεστεῖν; ἀγρυπνῆσαι δεῖ, πονῆσαι,
ἀπὸ τῶν οἰκείων ἀπελθεῖν, ὑπὸ παιδαρίου κατα-
φρονηθῆναι, ὑπὸ τῶν ἀπαντώντων καταγελα-
σθῆναι, ἐν παντὶ ἧττον ἔχειν, ἐν τιμῇ, ἐν ἀρχῇ, ἐν
δίκῃ, ἐν πραγματίῳ παντί. ταῦτα ἐπίσκεψαι. εἰ θέλεις ἀντικαταλλάξασθαι τούτων ἀπάθειαν, ἐλευ-
θερίαν, ἀταραξίαν· εἰ δὲ μή, μὴ προσάγαγε. μὴ ὡς
τὰ παιδία νῦν φιλόσοφος, ὕστερον δὲ τελώνης,
εἶτα ῥήτωρ, εἶτα ἐπίτροπος Καίσαρος. ταῦτα οὐ
συμφωνεῖ. ἕνα σε δεῖ ἄνθρωπον ἢ ἀγαθὸν ἢ κακὸν εἶναι· ἢ τὸ ἡγεμονικόν σε δεῖ ἐξεργάζεσθαι τὸ
σαυτοῦ ἢ τὸ ἐκτὸς ἢ περὶ τὰ ἔσω φιλοτεχνεῖν ἢ
περὶ τὰ ἔξω· τοῦτ' ἔστιν ἢ φιλοσόφου τάξιν ἐπέ-
χειν ἢ ἰδιώτου.

taking; then look at your own powers and see if you can bear it. Do you want to compete in the pentathlon or in wrestling? Look to your arms, your thighs, see what your loins are like. For different men are born for different tasks. Do you suppose that if you do this you can live as you do now—eat and drink as you do now, indulge desire and discontent just as before? Nay, you must sit up late, work hard, abandon your own people, be looked down on by a mere slave, be ridiculed by those who meet you, get the worst of it in everything—in honour, in office, in justice, in every possible thing. This is what you have to consider: whether you are willing to pay this price for peace of mind, freedom, tranquillity. If not, do not come near; do not be, like the children, first a philosopher, then a tax-collector, then an orator, then one of Caesar's procurators. These callings do not agree. You must be one man, good or bad; you must develop either your Governing Principle, or your outward endowments; you must study either your inner man, or outward things—

30

Τὰ καθήκοντα ὡς ἐπίπαν ταῖς σχέσεσι παραμε-
τρεῖται. πατήρ ἐστιν· ὑπαγορεύεται ἐπιμελεῖσθαι,
παραχωρεῖν ἁπάντων, ἀνέχεσθαι λοιδοροῦντος,
παίοντος.

«ἀλλὰ πατὴρ κακός ἐστι».

μή τι οὖν πρὸς ἀγαθὸν πατέρα φύσει ᾠκειώ-
θης; ἀλλὰ πρὸς πατέρα.

«ὁ ἀδελφὸς ἀδικεῖ».

τήρει τοιγαροῦν τὴν τάξιν τὴν σεαυτοῦ πρὸς
αὐτὸν μηδὲ σκόπει, τί ἐκεῖνος ποιεῖ, ἀλλὰ τί σοὶ
ποιήσαντι κατὰ φύσιν ἡ σὴ ἕξει προαίρεσις· σὲ
γὰρ ἄλλος οὐ βλάψει, ἂν μὴ σὺ θέλῃς· τότε δὲ ἔσῃ
βεβλαμμένος, ὅταν ὑπολάβῃς βλάπτεσθαι. οὕτως
οὖν ἀπὸ τοῦ γείτονος, ἀπὸ τοῦ πολίτου, ἀπὸ τοῦ
στρατηγοῦ τὸ καθῆκον εὑρήσεις, ἐὰν τὰς σχέσεις
ἐθίζῃ θεωρεῖν.

in a word, you must choose between the position of a philosopher and that of a mere outsider.

30

Appropriate acts are in general measured by the relations they are concerned with. 'He is your father.' This means you are called on to take care of him, give way to him in all things, bear with him if he reviles or strikes you.

'But he is a bad father.'

Well, have you any natural claim to a good father? No, only to a father.

'My brother wrongs me.'

Be careful then to maintain the relation you hold to him, and do not consider what he does, but what you must do if your purpose is to keep in accord with nature. For no one shall harm you, without your consent; you will only be harmed, when you think you are harmed. You will only discover what is proper to expect from neighbour, citizen, or praetor, if you get into the habit of looking at the relations implied by each.

31

Τῆς περὶ τοὺς θεοὺς εὐσεβείας ἴσθι ὅτι τὸ κυριώ-
τατον ἐκεῖνό ἐστιν, ὀρθὰς ὑπολήψεις περὶ αὐτῶν
ἔχειν ὡς ὄντων καὶ διοικούντων τὰ ὅλα καλῶς
καὶ δικαίως καὶ σαυτὸν εἰς τοῦτο κατατεταχέναι,
τὸ πείθεσθαι αὐτοῖς καὶ εἴκειν πᾶσι τοῖς γινομέ-
νοις καὶ ἀκολουθεῖν ἑκόντα ὡς ὑπὸ τῆς ἀρίστης
γνώμης ἐπιτελουμένοις. οὕτω γὰρ οὐ μέμψῃ ποτὲ
τοὺς θεοὺς οὔτε ἐγκαλέσεις ὡς ἀμελούμενος.
ἄλλως δὲ οὐχ οἷόν τε τοῦτο γίνεσθαι, ἐὰν μὴ
ἄρῃς ἀπὸ τῶν οὐκ ἐφ' ἡμῖν καὶ ἐν τοῖς ἐφ' ἡμῖν
μόνοις θῇς τὸ ἀγαθὸν καὶ τὸ κακόν. ὡς, ἄν γέ τι
ἐκείνων ὑπολάβῃς ἀγαθὸν ἢ κακόν, πᾶσα ἀνάγκη, ὅταν ἀποτυγχάνῃς ὧν θέλεις καὶ περιπίπτῃς
οἷς μὴ θέλεις, μέμψασθαί σε καὶ μισεῖν τοὺς αἰτί-
ους. πέφυκε γὰρ πρὸς τοῦτο πᾶν ζῷον τὰ μὲν
βλαβερὰ φαινόμενα καὶ τὰ αἴτια αὐτῶν φεύγειν
καὶ ἐκτρέπεσθαι, τὰ δὲ ὠφέλιμα καὶ τὰ αἴτια
αὐτῶν μετιέναι τε καὶ τεθηπέναι. ἀμήχανον οὖν

31

For piety towards the gods know that the most
important thing is this: to have right opinions
about them—that they exist, and that they gov-
ern the universe well and justly—and to have set
yourself to obey them, and to give way to all that
happens, following events with a free will, in the
belief that they are fulfilled by the highest mind.
For thus you will never blame the gods, nor accuse them of neglecting you. But this you cannot
achieve, unless you apply your conception of
good and evil to those things only which are in
our power, and not to those which are out of our
power. For if you apply your notion of good or
evil to the latter, then, as soon as you fail to get
what you will to get or fail to avoid what you will
to avoid, you will be bound to blame and hate
those you hold responsible. For every living
creature has a natural tendency to avoid and
shun what seems harmful and all that causes it,
and to pursue and admire what is helpful and all
that causes it. It is not possible then for one who

βλάπτεσθαί τινα οἰόμενον χαίρειν τῷ δοκοῦντι βλάπτειν, ὥσπερ καὶ τὸ αὐτῇ τῇ βλάβῃ χαίρειν ἀδύνατον. ἔνθεν καὶ πατὴρ ὑπὸ υἱοῦ λοιδορεῖται, ὅταν τῶν δοκούντων ἀγαθῶν εἶναι τῷ παιδὶ μὴ μεταδιδῷ· καὶ Πολυνείκην καὶ Ἐτεοκλέα τοῦτ' ἐποίησε πολεμίους ἀλλήλοις τὸ ἀγαθὸν οἴεσθαι τὴν τυραννίδα. διὰ τοῦτο καὶ ὁ γεωργὸς λοιδορεῖ τοὺς θεούς, διὰ τοῦτο ὁ ναύτης, διὰ τοῦτο ὁ ἔμπορος, διὰ τοῦτο οἱ τὰς γυναῖκας καὶ τὰ τέκνα ἀπολλύντες. ὅπου γὰρ τὸ συμφέρον, ἐπεῖ καὶ τὸ εὐσεβές. ὥστε, ὅστις ἐπιμελεῖται τοῦ ὀρέγεσθαι ὡς δεῖ καὶ ἐκκλίνειν, ἐν τῷ αὐτῷ καὶ εὐσεβείας ἐπιμελεῖται. σπένδειν δὲ καὶ θύειν καὶ ἀπάρχεσθαι κατὰ τὰ πάτρια ἑκάστοτε προσήκει καθαρῶς καὶ μὴ ἐπισεσυρμένως μηδὲ ἀμελῶς μηδέ γε γλίσχρως μηδὲ ὑπὲρ δύναμιν.

thinks he is harmed to take pleasure in what he thinks is the author of the harm, any more than to take pleasure in the harm itself. That is why a father is reviled by his son, when he does not give his son a share of what the son regards as good things; thus Polynices and Eteocles were set at enmity with one another by thinking that a king's throne was a good thing. That is why the farmer, and the sailor, and the merchant, and those who lose wife or children revile the gods. For men's religion is bound up with their interest. Therefore he who makes it his concern rightly to direct his will to get and his will to avoid, is thereby making piety his concern. But it is proper on each occasion to make libation and sacrifice and to offer first-fruits according to the custom of our fathers, with purity and not in slovenly or careless fashion, without meanness and without extravagance.

32

Ὅταν μαντικῇ προσίῃς, μέμνησο, ὅτι, τί μὲν ἀ-
ποβήσεται, οὐκ οἶδας, ἀλλὰ ἥκεις ὡς παρὰ τοῦ
μάντεως αὐτὸ πευσόμενος, ὁποῖον δέ τι ἐστίν, ἐ-
λήλυθας εἰδώς, εἴπερ εἶ φιλόσοφος. εἰ γάρ ἐστί τι
τῶν οὐκ ἐφ᾽ ἡμῖν, πᾶσα ἀνάγκη μήτε ἀγαθὸν αὐτὸ
εἶναι μήτε κακόν. μὴ φέρε οὖν πρὸς τὸν μάντιν
ὄρεξιν ἢ ἔκκλισιν μηδὲ τρέμων αὐτῷ πρόσει,
ἀλλὰ διεγνωκώς, ὅτι πᾶν τὸ ἀποβησόμενον ἀδιά-
φορον καὶ οὐδὲν πρὸς σέ, ὁποῖον δ᾽ ἂν ᾖ, ἔσται
αὐτῷ χρήσασθαι καλῶς καὶ τοῦτο οὐθεὶς κωλύσει. θαρρῶν οὖν ὡς ἐπὶ συμβούλους ἔρχου τοὺς
θεούς· καὶ λοιπόν, ὅταν τί σοι συμβουλευθῇ, μέμνησο τίνας συμβούλους παρέλαβες καὶ τίνων
παρακούσεις ἀπειθήσας. ἔρχου δὲ ἐπὶ τὸ μαντεύεσθαι, καθάπερ ἠξίου Σωκράτης, ἐφ᾽ ὧν ἡ πᾶσα
σκέψις τὴν ἀναφορὰν εἰς τὴν ἔκβασιν ἔχει καὶ
οὔτε ἐκ λόγου οὔτε ἐκ τέχνης τινὸς ἄλλης ἀφορ-
μαὶ δίδονται πρὸς τὸ συνιδεῖν τὸ προκείμενον·

32

When you make use of prophecy remember that while you know not what the issue will be, but are come to learn it from the prophet, you do know before you come what manner of thing it is, if you are really a philosopher. For if the event is not in our control, it cannot be either good or evil. Therefore do not bring with you to the prophet the will to get or the will to avoid, and do not approach him with trembling, but with your mind made up, that the whole issue is indifferent and does not affect you and that, whatever it be, it will be in your power to make good use of it, and no one shall hinder this. With confidence then approach the gods as counsellors, and further, when the counsel is given you, remember whose counsel it is, and whom you will be disregarding if you disobey. And consult the oracle, as Socrates thought men should, only when the whole question turns upon the issue of events, and neither reason nor any art of man provides opportunities for discovering what lies before you. Therefore,

ὥστε, ὅταν δεήσῃ συγκινδυνεῦσαι φίλῳ ἢ πατρίδι, μὴ μαντεύεσθαι, εἰ συγκινδυνευτέον. καὶ
γὰρ ἂν προείπῃ σοι ὁ μάντις φαῦλα γεγονέναι τὰ
ἱερά, δῆλον ὅτι θάνατος σημαίνεται ἢ πήρωσις
μέρους τινὸς τοῦ σώματος ἢ φυγή· ἀλλ᾽ αἱρεῖ ὁ
λόγος καὶ σὺν τούτοις παρίστασθαι τῷ φίλῳ καὶ
τῇ πατρίδι συγκινδυνεύειν. τοιγαροῦν τῷ μείζονι
μάντει πρόσεχε, τῷ Πυθίῳ, ὃς ἐξέβαλε τοῦ ναοῦ
τὸν οὐ βοηθήσαντα ἀναιρουμένῳ τῷ φίλῳ.

33

Τάξον τινὰ ἤδη χαρακτῆρα σαυτῷ καὶ τύπον, ὃν
φυλάξεις ἐπί τε σεαυτοῦ ὢν καὶ ἀνθρώποις ἐν-
τυγχάνων. καὶ σιωπῇ τὸ πολὺ ἔστω ἢ λαλείσθω τὰ
ἀναγκαῖα καὶ δι᾽ ὀλίγων. σπανίως δέ ποτε καιροῦ
παρακαλοῦντος ἐπὶ τὸ λέγειν λέξον μέν, ἀλλὰ περὶ οὐδενὸς τῶν τυχόντων· μὴ περὶ μονομαχιῶν, μὴ
περὶ ἱπποδρομιῶν, μὴ περὶ ἀθλητῶν, μὴ περὶ βρω-
μάτων ἢ πομάτων, τῶν ἑκασταχοῦ, μάλιστα δὲ μὴ

when it is your duty to risk your life with friend or country, do not ask the oracle whether you should risk your life. For if the prophet warns you that the sacrifice is unfavourable, though it is plain that this means death or exile or injury to some part of your body, yet reason requires that even at this cost you must stand by your friend and share your country's danger. Wherefore pay heed to the greater prophet, Pythian Apollo, who cast out of his temple the man who did not help his friend when he was being killed.[1]

33

Lay down for yourself from the first a definite stamp and style of conduct, which you will maintain when you are alone and also in the society of men. Be silent for the most part, or, if you speak,

---

1. Aelian, Var. Hist., tells how three men sent to Delphi had an encounter with robbers. One ran away, another accidentally killed the third in trying to defend him. The Oracle would have nothing to say to the runaway, and absolved the homicide.

περὶ ἀνθρώπων ψέγων ἢ ἐπαινῶν ἢ συγκρίνων. ἂν
μὲν οὖν οἷός τε ᾖς, μετάγαγε τοῖς σοῖς λόγοις καὶ
τοὺς τῶν συνόντων ἐπὶ τὸ προσῆκον. εἰ δὲ ἐν ἀλ-
λοφύλοις ἀποληφθεὶς τύχοις, σιῶπα. γέλως μὴ
πολὺς ἔστω μηδὲ ἐπὶ πολλοῖς μηδὲ ἀνειμένος.

ὅρκον παραίτησαι, εἰ μὲν οἷόν τε, εἰς ἅπαν, εἰ
δὲ μή, ἐκ τῶν ἐνόντων. ἑστιάσεις τὰς ἔξω καὶ
ἰδιωτικὰς διακρούου· ἐὰν δέ ποτε γίνηται καιρός,
ἐντετάσθω σοι ἡ προσοχή, μήποτε ἄρα ὑπορρυῇς
εἰς ἰδιωτισμόν. ἴσθι γάρ, ὅτι, ἐὰν ὁ ἑταῖρος ᾖ μεμο-
λυσμένος, καὶ τὸν συνανατριβόμενον αὐτῷ συμ-
μολύνεσθαι ἀνάγκη, κἂν αὐτὸς ὢν τύχῃ καθαρός.

τὰ περὶ τὸ σῶμα μέχρι τῆς χρείας ψιλῆς παρα-
λάμβανε, οἷον τροφάς, πόμα, ἀμπεχόνην, οἰκίαν,
οἰκετίαν· τὸ δὲ πρὸς δόξαν ἢ τρυφὴν ἅπαν περί-
γραφε.

περὶ ἀφροδίσια εἰς δύναμιν πρὸ γάμου καθα-
ρευτέον· ἁπτομένῳ δὲ ὧν νόμιμόν ἐστι μεταλη-
πτέον. μὴ μέντοι ἐπαχθὴς γίνου τοῖς χρωμένοις

say only what is necessary and in a few words. Talk, but rarely, if occasion calls you, but do not talk of ordinary things—of gladiators, or horse-races, or athletes, or of meats or drinks—these are topics that arise everywhere—but above all do not talk about men in blame or compliment or comparison. If you can, turn the conversation of your company by your talk to some fitting subject; but if you should chance to be isolated among strangers, be silent. Do not laugh much, nor at many things, nor without restraint.

Refuse to take oaths, altogether if that be possible, but if not, as far as circumstances allow. Refuse the entertainments of strangers and the vulgar. But if occasion arise to accept them, then strain every nerve to avoid lapsing into the state of the vulgar. For know that, if your comrade have a stain on him, he that associates with him must needs share the stain, even though he be clean in himself.

For your body take just so much as your bare need requires, such as food, drink, clothing,

μηδὲ ἐλεγκτικός· μηδὲ πολλαχοῦ τὸ ὅτι αὐτὸς οὐ
χρῇ, παράφερε. ἐὰν τίς σοι ἀπαγγείλῃ ὅτι ὁ δεῖνά
σε κακῶς λέγει, μὴ ἀπολογοῦ πρὸς τὰ λεχθέντα,
ἀλλ᾽ ἀποκρίνου διότι «ἠγνόει γὰρ τὰ ἄλλα τὰ προ-
σόντα μοι κακά, ἐπεὶ οὐκ ἂν ταῦτα μόνα ἔλεγεν».

εἰς τὰ θέατρα τὸ πολὺ παριέναι οὐκ ἀναγκαῖ-
ον. εἰ δέ ποτε καιρὸς εἴη, μηδενὶ σπουδάζων φαίνου ἢ σεαυτῷ, τοῦτ᾽ ἔστι. θέλε γίνεσθαι μόνα τὰ
γινόμενα καὶ νικᾶν μόνον τὸν νικῶντα· οὕτω γὰρ
οὐκ ἐμποδισθήσῃ. βοῆς δὲ καὶ τοῦ ἐπιγελᾶν τινι ἢ
ἐπὶ πολὺ συγκινεῖσθαι παντελῶς ἀπέχου. καὶ μετὰ
τὸ ἀπαλλαγῆναι μὴ πολλὰ περὶ τῶν γεγενημένων
διαλέγου, ὅσα μὴ φέρει πρὸς τὴν σὴν ἐπανόρθω-
σιν· ἐμφαίνεται γὰρ ἐκ τοῦ τοιούτου, ὅτι ἐθαύμα-
σας τὴν θέαν.

εἰς ἀκροάσεις τινῶν μὴ εἰκῇ μηδὲ ῥᾳδίως πά-
ριθι· παριὼν δὲ τὸ σεμνὸν καὶ τὸ εὐσταθὲς καὶ
ἅμα ἀνεπαχθὲς φύλασσε. ὅταν τινὶ μέλλῃς συμ-
βαλεῖν, μάλιστα τῶν ἐν ὑπεροχῇ δοκούντων, πρό-

house, servants, but cut down all that tends to luxury and outward show.

Avoid impurity to the utmost of your power before marriage, and if you indulge your passion, let it be done lawfully. But do not be offensive or censorious to those who indulge it, and do not be always bringing up your own chastity. If someone tells you that so-and-so speaks ill of you, do not defend yourself against what he says, but answer, 'He did not know my other faults, or he would not have mentioned these alone.'

It is not necessary for the most part to go to the games; but if you should have occasion to go, show that your first concern is for yourself; that is, wish that only to happen which does happen, and him only to win who does win, for so you will suffer no hindrance. But refrain entirely from applause, or ridicule, or prolonged excitement. And when you go away do not talk much of what happened there, except so far as it tends to your improvement. For to talk about it implies that the spectacle excited your wonder.

βαλε σαυτῷ, τί ἂν ἐποίησεν ἐν τούτῳ Σωκράτης ἢ Ζήνων, καὶ οὐκ ἀπορήσεις τοῦ χρήσασθαι προση-κόντως τῷ ἐμπεσόντι.

ὅταν φοιτᾷς πρός τινα τῶν μέγα δυναμένων, πρόβαλε, ὅτι οὐχ εὑρήσεις αὐτὸν ἔνδον, ὅτι ἀπο-κλεισθήσῃ, ὅτι ἐντιναχθήσονταί σοι αἱ θύραι, ὅτι οὐ φροντιεῖ σου. κἂν σὺν τούτοις ἐλθεῖν καθήκῃ, ἐλθὼν φέρε τὰ γινόμενα καὶ μηδέποτε εἴπῃς αὐ-τὸς πρὸς ἑαυτὸν ὅτι «οὐκ ἦν τοσούτου»· ἰδιω-τικὸν γὰρ καὶ διαβεβλημένον πρὸς τὰ ἐκτός.

ἐν ταῖς ὁμιλίαις ἀπέστω τὸ ἑαυτοῦ τινων ἔρ-γων ἢ κινδύνων ἐπὶ πολὺ καὶ ἀμέτρως μεμνῆσθαι. οὐ γάρ, ὡς σοὶ ἡδύ ἐστι τὸ τῶν σῶν κινδύνων με-μνῆσθαι, οὕτω καὶ τοῖς ἄλλοις ἡδύ ἐστι τὸ τῶν σοὶ συμβεβηκότων ἀκούειν.

ἀπέστω δὲ καὶ τὸ γέλωτα κινεῖν· ὀλισθηρὸς γὰρ ὁ τρόπος εἰς ἰδιωτισμὸν καὶ ἅμα ἱκανὸς τὴν αἰδῶ τὴν πρὸς σὲ τῶν πλησίον ἀνιέναι.

ἐπισφαλὲς δὲ καὶ τὸ εἰς αἰσχρολογίαν προελ-

Do not go lightly or casually to hear lectures; but if you do go, maintain your gravity and dignity and do not make yourself offensive. When you are going to meet anyone, and particularly some man of reputed eminence, set before your mind the thought, 'What would Socrates or Zeno have done?' and you will not fail to make proper use of the occasion.

When you go to visit some great man, prepare your mind by thinking that you will not find him in, that you will be shut out, that the doors will be slammed in your face, that he will pay no heed to you. And if in spite of all this you find it fitting for you to go, go and bear what happens and never say to yourself, 'It was not worth all this'; for that shows a vulgar mind and one at odds with outward things.

In your conversation avoid frequent and disproportionate mention of your own doings or adventures; for other people do not take the same pleasure in hearing what has happened to you as you take in recounting your adventures.

θεῖν. ὅταν οὖν τι συμβῇ τοιοῦτον, ἂν μὲν εὔκαι-
ρον ᾖ, καὶ ἐπίπληξον τῷ προελθόντι· εἰ δὲ μή, τῷ
γε ἀποσιωπῆσαι καὶ ἐρυθριᾶσαι καὶ σκυθρωπάσαι
δῆλος γίνου δυσχεραίνων τῷ λόγῳ.

34

Ὅταν ἡδονῆς τινος φαντασίαν λάβῃς, καθάπερ
ἐπὶ τῶν ἄλλων, φύλασσε σαυτόν, μὴ συναρπα-
σθῇς ὑπ᾽ αὐτῆς· ἀλλ᾽ ἐκδεξάσθω σε τὸ πρᾶγμα,
καὶ ἀναβολήν τινα παρὰ σεαυτοῦ λάβε. ἔπειτα
μνήσθητι ἀμφοτέρων τῶν χρόνων, καθ᾽ ὅν τε ἀ-
πολαύσεις τῆς ἡδονῆς, καὶ καθ᾽ ὃν ἀπολαύσας
ὕστερον μετανοήσεις καὶ αὐτὸς σεαυτῷ λοιδο-
ρήσῃ· καὶ τούτοις ἀντίθες ὅπως ἀποσχόμενος
χαιρήσεις καὶ ἐπαινέσεις αὐτὸς σεαυτόν. ἐὰν δέ
σοι καιρὸς φανῇ ἅψασθαι τοῦ ἔργου, πρόσεχε, μὴ
ἡττήσῃ σε τὸ προσηνὲς αὐτοῦ καὶ ἡδὺ καὶ ἐπαγω-
γόν· ἀλλ᾽ ἀντιτίθει, πόσῳ ἄμεινον τὸ συνειδέναι
σεαυτῷ ταύτην τὴν νίκην νενικηκότι.

Avoid raising men's laughter; for it is a habit that easily slips into vulgarity, and it may well suffice to lessen your neighbour's respect.

It is dangerous too to lapse into foul language; when anything of the kind occurs, rebuke the offender, if the occasion allow, and if not, make it plain to him by your silence, or a blush or a frown, that you are angry at his words.

34

When you imagine some pleasure, beware that it does not carry you away, like other imaginations. Wait a while, and give yourself pause. Next remember two things: how long you will enjoy the pleasure, and also how long you will afterwards repent and revile yourself. And set on the other side the joy and self-satisfaction you will feel if you refrain. And if the moment seems come to realize it, take heed that you be not overcome by the winning sweetness and attraction of it; set in the other scale the thought how much better is the consciousness of having vanquished it.

35

Ὅταν τι διαγνούς, ὅτι ποιητέον ἐστί, ποιῇς, μηδέποτε φύγῃς ὀφθῆναι πράσσων αὐτό, κἂν ἀλλοῖόν
τι μέλλωσιν οἱ πολλοὶ περὶ αὐτοῦ ὑπολαμβάνειν.
εἰ μὲν γὰρ οὐκ ὀρθῶς ποιεῖς, αὐτὸ τὸ ἔργον φεῦ-
γε· εἰ δὲ ὀρθῶς, τί φοβῇ τοὺς ἐπιπλήξοντας οὐκ
ὀρθῶς;

36

Ὡς τὸ «ἡμέρα ἐστί» καὶ «νύξ ἐστι» πρὸς μὲν τὸ
διεζευγμένον μεγάλην ἔχει ἀξίαν, πρὸς δὲ τὸ συμπεπλεγμένον ἀπαξίαν, οὕτω καὶ τὸ τὴν μείζω με-
ρίδα ἐκλέξασθαι πρὸς μὲν τὸ σῶμα ἐχέτω ἀξίαν,
πρὸς δὲ τὸ κοινωνικὸν ἐν ἑστιάσει, οἷον δεῖ, φυλάξαι, ἀπαξίαν ἔχει. ὅταν οὖν συνεσθίῃς ἑτέρῳ,
μέμνησο, μὴ μόνον τὴν πρὸς τὸ σῶμα ἀξίαν τῶν
παρακειμένων ὁρᾶν, ἀλλὰ καὶ τὴν πρὸς τὸν
ἑστιάτορα αἰδῶ φυλάξαι.

35

When you do a thing because you have determined that it ought to be done, never avoid being seen doing it, even if the opinion of the multitude is going to condemn you. For if your action is wrong, then avoid doing it altogether, but if it is right, why do you fear those who will rebuke you wrongly?

36

The phrases, 'It is day' and 'It is night', mean a great deal if taken separately, but have no meaning if combined. In the same way, to choose the larger portion at a banquet may be worthwhile for your body, but if you want to maintain social decencies it is worthless. Therefore, when you are at meat with another, remember not only to consider the value of what is set before you for the body, but also to maintain your self-respect before your host.

37

Ἐὰν ὑπὲρ δύναμιν ἀναλάβῃς τι πρόσωπον, καὶ ἐν
τούτῳ ἠσχημόνησας καί, ὃ ἠδύνασο ἐκπληρῶσαι,
παρέλιπες.

38

Ἐν τῷ περιπατεῖν καθάπερ προσέχεις, μὴ ἐπιβῇς
ἥλῳ ἢ στρέψῃς τὸν πόδα σου, οὕτω πρόσεχε, μὴ
καὶ τὸ ἡγεμονικὸν βλάψῃς τὸ σεαυτοῦ. καὶ τοῦτο
ἐὰν ἐφ᾽ ἑκάστου ἔργου παραφυλάσσωμεν, ἀσφαλέστερον ἁψόμεθα τοῦ ἔργου.

39

Μέτρον κτήσεως τὸ σῶμα ἑκάστῳ ὡς ὁ ποὺς
ὑποδήματος. ἐὰν μὲν οὖν ἐπὶ τούτου στῇς, φυλάξεις τὸ μέτρον· ἐὰν δὲ ὑπερβῇς, ὡς κατὰ κρημνοῦ
λοιπὸν ἀνάγκη φέρεσθαι· καθάπερ καὶ ἐπὶ τοῦ
ὑποδήματος, ἐὰν ὑπὲρ τὸν πόδα ὑπερβῇς, γίνεται
κατάχρυσον ὑπόδημα, εἶτα πορφυροῦν, κεντητόν.
τοῦ γὰρ ἅπαξ ὑπὲρ τὸ μέτρον ὅρος οὐθείς ἐστιν.

37

If you try to act a part beyond your powers, you not only disgrace yourself in it, but you neglect the part which you could have filled with success.

38

As in walking you take care not to tread on a nail or to twist your foot, so take care that you do not harm your Governing Principle. And if we guard this in everything we do, we shall set to work more securely.

39

Every man's body is a measure for his property, as the foot is the measure for his shoe. If you stick to this limit, you will keep the right measure; if you go beyond it, you are bound to be carried away down a precipice in the end; just as with the shoe, if you once go beyond the foot, your shoe puts on gilding, and soon purple and embroidery. For when once you go beyond the measure there is no limit.

40

Αἱ γυναῖκες εὐθὺς ἀπὸ τεσσαρεσκαίδεκα ἐτῶν ὑπὸ τῶν ἀνδρῶν κυρίαι καλοῦνται. τοιγαροῦν ὁρῶσαι, ὅτι ἄλλο μὲν οὐδὲν αὐταῖς πρόσεστι, μόνον δὲ συγκοιμῶνται τοῖς ἀνδράσι, ἄρχονται καλλωπίζεσθαι καὶ ἐν τούτῳ πάσας ἔχειν τὰς ἐλπίδας. προσέχειν οὖν ἄξιον, ἵνα αἴσθωνται, διότι ἐπ᾽ οὐδενὶ ἄλλῳ τιμῶνται ἢ τῷ κόσμιαι φαίνεσθαι καὶ αἰδήμονες.

41

Ἀφυΐας σημεῖον τὸ ἐνδιατρίβειν τοῖς περὶ τὸ σῶμα, οἷον ἐπὶ πολὺ γυμνάζεσθαι, ἐπὶ πολὺ ἐσθίειν, ἐπὶ πολὺ πίνειν, ἐπὶ πολὺ ἀποπατεῖν, ὀχεύειν. ἀλλὰ ταῦτα μὲν ἐν παρέργῳ ποιητέον· περὶ δὲ τὴν γνώμην ἡ πᾶσα ἔστω ἐπιστροφή.

40

Women from fourteen years upwards are called 'madam' by men. Wherefore, when they see that the only advantage they have got is to be marriageable, they begin to make themselves smart and to set all their hopes on this. We must take pains then to make them understand that they are really honoured for nothing but a modest and decorous life.

41

It is a sign of a dull mind to dwell upon the cares of the body, to prolong exercise, eating, drinking, and other bodily functions. These things are to be done by the way; all your attention must be given to the mind.

42

Ὅταν σέ τις κακῶς ποιῇ ἢ κακῶς λέγῃ, μέμνησο,
ὅτι καθήκειν αὐτῷ οἰόμενος ποιεῖ ἢ λέγει. οὐχ
οἷόν τε οὖν ἀκολουθεῖν αὐτὸν τῷ σοὶ φαινομένῳ,
ἀλλὰ τῷ ἑαυτῷ, ὥστε, εἰ κακῶς αὐτῷ φαίνεται,
ἐκεῖνος βλάπτεται, ὅστις καὶ ἐξηπάτηται. καὶ γὰρ
τὸ ἀληθὲς συμπεπλεγμένον ἄν τις ὑπολάβῃ ψεῦδος, οὐ τὸ συμπεπλεγμένον βέβλαπται, ἀλλ᾽ ὁ
ἐξαπατηθείς. ἀπὸ τούτων οὖν ὁρμώμενος πρᾴως
ἕξεις πρὸς τὸν λοιδοροῦντα. ἐπιφθέγγου γὰρ ἐφ᾽
ἑκάστῳ ὅτι «ἔδοξεν αὐτῷ».

43

Πᾶν πρᾶγμα δύο ἔχει λαβάς, τὴν μὲν φορητήν,
τὴν δὲ ἀφόρητον. ὁ ἀδελφὸς ἐὰν ἀδικῇ, ἐντεῦθεν
αὐτὸ μὴ λάμβανε, ὅτι ἀδικεῖ (αὕτη γὰρ ἡ λαβή
ἐστιν αὐτοῦ οὐ φορητή), ἀλλὰ ἐκεῖθεν μᾶλλον, ὅ-
τι ἀδελφός, ὅτι σύντροφος, καὶ λήψῃ αὐτὸ καθ᾽ ὃ
φορητόν.

42

When a man speaks evil or does evil to you, re-member that he does or says it because he thinks it is fitting for him. It is not possible for him to follow what seems good to you, but only what seems good to him, so that, if his opinion is wrong, he suffers, in that he is the victim of de-ception. In the same way, if a composite judge-ment which is true is thought to be false, it is not the judgement that suffers, but the man who is deluded about it. If you act on this principle you will be gentle to him who reviles you, saying to yourself on each occasion, 'He thought it right.'

43

Everything has two handles, one by which you can carry it, the other by which you cannot. If your brother wrongs you, do not take it by that handle, the handle of his wrong, for you cannot carry it by that, but rather by the other handle—that he is a brother, brought up with you, and then you will take it by the handle that you can carry by.

44

Οὗτοι οἱ λόγοι ἀσύνακτοι «ἐγώ σου πλουσιώτερός εἰμι, ἐγώ σου ἄρα κρείσσων»· «ἐγώ σου λογιώτερος, ἐγώ σου ἄρα κρείσσων». ἐκεῖνοι δὲ
μᾶλλον συνακτικοί «ἐγώ σου πλουσιώτερός εἰμι,
ἡ ἐμὴ ἄρα κτῆσις τῆς σῆς κρείσσων»· «ἐγώ σου
λογιώτερος, ἡ ἐμὴ ἄρα λέξις τῆς σῆς κρείσσων».
σὺ δέ γε οὔτε κτῆσις εἶ οὔτε λέξις.

45

Λούεταί τις ταχέως· μὴ εἴπῃς ὅτι κακῶς, ἀλλ᾽ ὅτι
ταχέως. πίνει τις πολὺν οἶνον· μὴ εἴπῃς ὅτι κακῶς,
ἀλλ᾽ ὅτι πολύν. πρὶν γὰρ διαγνῶναι τὸ δόγμα,
πόθεν οἶσθα, εἰ κακῶς; οὕτως οὐ συμβήσεταί σοι
ἄλλων μὲν φαντασίας καταληπτικὰς λαμβάνειν,
ἄλλοις δὲ συγκατατίθεσθαι.

44

It is illogical to reason thus, 'I am richer than you, therefore I am superior to you', 'I am more eloquent than you, therefore I am superior to you.' It is more logical to reason, 'I am richer than you, therefore my property is superior to yours', 'I am more eloquent than you, therefore my speech is superior to yours.' You are something more than property or speech.

45

If a man wash quickly, do not say that he washes badly, but that he washes quickly. If a man drink much wine, do not say that he drinks badly, but that he drinks much. For till you have decided what judgement prompts him, how do you know that he acts badly? If you do as I say, you will assent to your apprehensive impressions and to none other.

46

Μηδαμοῦ σεαυτὸν εἴπῃς φιλόσοφον μηδὲ λάλει
τὸ πολὺ ἐν ἰδιώταις περὶ τῶν θεωρημάτων, ἀλλὰ
ποίει τὸ ἀπὸ τῶν θεωρημάτων· οἷον ἐν συμποσίῳ
μὴ λέγε, πῶς δεῖ ἐσθίειν, ἀλλ᾽ ἔσθιε, ὡς δεῖ. μέμνησο γάρ, ὅτι οὕτως ἀφῃρήκει πανταχόθεν Σωκράτης τὸ ἐπιδεικτικόν, ὥστε ἤρχοντο πρὸς
αὐτὸν βουλόμενοι φιλοσόφοις ὑπ᾽ αὐτοῦ συ-
σταθῆναι, κἀκεῖνος ἀπῆγεν αὐτούς. οὕτως ἠνεί-
χετο παρορώμενος. κἂν περὶ θεωρήματός τινος
ἐν ἰδιώταις ἐμπίπτῃ λόγος, σιώπα τὸ πολύ· μέγας
γὰρ ὁ κίνδυνος εὐθὺς ἐξεμέσαι, ὃ οὐκ ἔπεψας. καὶ
ὅταν εἴπῃ σοί τις, ὅτι οὐδὲν οἶσθα, καὶ σὺ μὴ δη-
χθῇς, τότε ἴσθι, ὅτι ἄρχῃ τοῦ ἔργου. ἐπεὶ καὶ τὰ
πρόβατα οὐ χόρτον φέροντα τοῖς ποιμέσιν ἐπι-
δεικνύει πόσον, ἔφαγεν, ἀλλὰ τὴν νομὴν ἔσω πέ-
ψαντα ἔρια ἔξω φέρει καὶ γάλα· καὶ σὺ τοίνυν μὴ
τὰ θεωρήματα τοῖς ἰδιώταις ἐπιδείκνυε, ἀλλ᾽ ἀπ᾽
αὐτῶν πεφθέντων τὰ ἔργα.

46

On no occasion call yourself a philosopher, nor talk at large of your principles among the multitude, but act on your principles. For instance, at a banquet do not say how one ought to eat, but eat as you ought. Remember that Socrates had so completely got rid of the thought of display that when men came and wanted an introduction to philosophers he took them to be introduced; so patient of neglect was he. And if a discussion arise among the multitude on some principle, keep silent for the most part; for you are in great danger of blurting out some undigested thought. And when someone says to you, 'You know nothing', and you do not let it provoke you, then know that you are really on the right road. For sheep do not bring grass to their shepherds and show them how much they have eaten, but they digest their fodder and then produce it in the form of wool and milk. Do the same yourself; instead of displaying your principles to the multitude, show them the results of the principles you have digested.

47

Ὅταν εὐτελῶς ἡρμοσμένος ἦς κατὰ τὸ σῶμα, μὴ καλλωπίζου ἐπὶ τούτῳ μήδ᾽, ἂν ὕδωρ πίνῃς, ἐκ πάσης ἀφορμῆς λέγε, ὅτι ὕδωρ πίνεις. κἂν ἀ- σκῆσαί ποτε πρὸς πόνον θέλῃς. σεαυτῷ καὶ μὴ τοῖς ἔξω· μὴ τοὺς ἀνδριάντας περιλάμβανε· ἀλλὰ διψῶν ποτε σφοδρῶς ἐπίσπασαι ψυχροῦ ὕδατος καὶ ἔκπτυσον καὶ μηδενὶ εἴπῃς.

48

Ἰδιώτου στάσις καὶ χαρακτήρ· οὐδέποτε ἐξ ἑαυ- τοῦ προσδοκᾷ ὠφέλειαν ἢ βλάβην, ἀλλ᾽ ἀπὸ τῶν ἔξω. φιλοσόφου στάσις καὶ χαρακτήρ· πᾶσαν ὠφέλειαν καὶ βλάβην ἐξ ἑαυτοῦ προσδοκᾷ.

σημεῖα προκόπτοντος· οὐδένα ψέγει, οὐδένα ἐπαινεῖ, οὐδένα μέμφεται, οὐδενὶ ἐγκαλεῖ, οὐδὲν περὶ ἑαυτοῦ λέγει ὡς ὄντος τινὸς ἢ εἰδότος τι. ὅταν ἐμποδισθῇ τι ἢ κωλυθῇ, ἑαυτῷ ἐγκαλεῖ. κἂν τις αὐτὸν ἐπαινῇ, καταγελᾷ τοῦ ἐπαινοῦντος αὐ-

47

When you have adopted the simple life, do not pride yourself upon it, and if you are a water-drinker do not say on every occasion, 'I am a water-drinker.' And if you ever want to train laboriously, keep it to yourself and do not make a show of it. Do not embrace statues. If you are very thirsty take a good draught of cold water, and rinse you mouth and tell no one.

48

The ignorant man's position and character is this: he never looks to himself for benefit or harm, but to the world outside him. The philosopher's position and character is that he always look to himself for benefit and harm.

The signs of one who is making progress are: he blames none, praises none, complains of none, accuses none, never speaks of himself as if he were somebody, or as if he knew anything. And if anyone compliments him he laughs in himself at his compliment; and if one blames him, he makes no

τὸς παρ' ἑαυτῷ· κἂν ψέγῃ, οὐκ ἀπολογεῖται. περί-
εισι δὲ καθάπερ οἱ ἄρρωστοι, εὐλαβούμενός τι
κινῆσαι τῶν καθισταμένων, πρὶν πῆξιν λαβεῖν.
ὄρεξιν ἅπασαν ἦρκεν ἐξ ἑαυτοῦ· τὴν δ' ἔκκλισιν
εἰς μόνα τὰ παρὰ φύσιν τῶν ἐφ' ἡμῖν μετατέθει-
κεν. ὁρμῇ πρὸς ἅπαντα ἀνειμένῃ χρῆται. ἂν ἠλίθιος ἢ ἀμαθὴς δοκῇ, οὐ πεφρόντικεν. ἑνί τε λόγῳ,
ὡς ἐχθρὸν ἑαυτὸν παραφυλάσσει καὶ ἐπίβουλον.

49

Ὅταν τις ἐπὶ τῷ νοεῖν καὶ ἐξηγεῖσθαι δύνασθαι τὰ
Χρυσίππου βιβλία σεμνύνηται, λέγε αὐτὸς πρὸς
ἑαυτὸν ὅτι «εἰ μὴ Χρύσιππος ἀσαφῶς ἐγεγράφει,
οὐδὲν ἂν εἶχεν οὗτος, ἐφ' ᾧ ἐσεμνύνετο».

ἐγὼ δὲ τί βούλομαι; καταμαθεῖν τὴν φύσιν καὶ
ταύτῃ ἕπεσθαι. ζητῶ οὖν, τίς ἐστιν ὁ ἐξηγούμενος·
καὶ ἀκούσας, ὅτι Χρύσιππος, ἔρχομαι πρὸς αὐτόν.
ἀλλ' οὐ νοῶ τὰ γεγραμμένα· ζητῶ οὖν τὸν ἐξηγούμενον. καὶ μέχρι τούτων οὔπω σεμνὸν οὐδέν.

defence. He goes about like a convalescent, careful not to disturb his constitution on its road to recovery, until it has got firm hold. He has got rid of the will to get, and his will to avoid is directed no longer to what is beyond our power but only to what is in our power and contrary to nature. In all things he exercises his will without strain. If men regard him as foolish or ignorant he pays no heed. In one word, he keeps watch and guard on himself as his own enemy, lying in wait for him.

49

When a man prides himself on being able to understand and interpret the books of Chrysippus, say to yourself, 'If Chrysippus had not written obscurely this man would have had nothing on which to pride himself.'

What is my object? To understand Nature and follow her. I look then for someone who interprets her, and having heard that Chrysippus does I come to him. But I do not understand his writings, so I seek an interpreter. So far there is noth-

ὅταν δὲ εὕρω τὸν ἐξηγούμενον, ἀπολείπεται χρῆσθαι τοῖς παρηγγελμένοις· τοῦτο αὐτὸ μόνον σεμνόν ἐστιν. ἂν δὲ αὐτὸ τοῦτο τὸ ἐξηγεῖσθαι θαυμάσω, τί ἄλλο ἢ γραμματικὸς ἀπετελέσθην ἀντὶ φιλοσόφου; πλήν γε δὴ ὅτι ἀντὶ Ὁμήρου Χρύσιππον ἐξηγούμενος. μᾶλλον οὖν, ὅταν τις εἴπῃ μοι «ἐπανάγνωθί μοι Χρύσιππον», ἐρυθριῶ, ὅταν μὴ δύνωμαι ὅμοια τὰ ἔργα καὶ σύμφωνα ἐπιδεικνύειν τοῖς λόγοις.

50

Ὅσα προτίθεται, τούτοις ὡς νόμοις, ὡς ἀσεβήσων, ἂν παραβῇς, ἔμμενε. ὅ τι δ’ ἂν ἐρῇ τις περὶ σοῦ, μὴ ἐπιστρέφου· τοῦτο γὰρ οὐκ ἔτ’ ἔστι σόν.

51

Εἰς ποῖον ἔτι χρόνον ἀναβάλλῃ τὸ τῶν βελτίστων ἀξιοῦν σεαυτὸν καὶ ἐν μηδενὶ παραβαίνειν τὸν διαιροῦντα λόγον; παρείληφας τὰ θεωρή-

ing to be proud of. But when I have found the interpreter it remains for me to act on his precepts;
that and that alone is a thing to be proud of. But
if I admire the mere power of exposition, it
comes to this—that I am turned into a grammar-
ian instead of a philosopher, except that I interpret Chrysippus in place of Homer. Therefore,
when someone says to me, 'Read me Chrysippus',
when I cannot point to actions which are in harmony and correspondence with his teaching, I
am rather inclined to blush.

50

Whatever principles you put before you, hold fast
to them as laws which it will be impious to transgress. But pay no heed to what anyone says of you;
for this is something beyond your own control.

51

How long will you wait to think yourself worthy
of the highest and transgress in nothing the clear
pronouncement of reason? You have received the

ματα, οἷς ἔδει σε συμβάλλειν, καὶ συμβέβληκας. ποῖον οὖν ἔτι διδάσκαλον προσδοκᾷς, ἵνα εἰς ἐκεῖνον ὑπερθῇ τὴν ἐπανόρθωσιν ποιῆσαι τὴν σεαυτοῦ; οὐκ ἔτι εἶ μειράκιον, ἀλλὰ ἀνὴρ ἤδη τέλειος. ἂν νῦν ἀμελήσῃς καὶ ῥαθυμήσῃς καὶ ἀεὶ προθέσεις ἐκ προθέσεως ποιῇ καὶ ἡμέρας ἄλλας ἐπ᾽ ἄλλαις ὁρίζῃς, μεθ᾽ ἃς προσέξεις σεαυτῷ, λήσεις σεαυτὸν οὐ προκόψας, ἀλλ᾽ ἰδιώτης διατελέσεις καὶ ζῶν καὶ ἀποθνῄσκων. ἤδη οὖν ἀξίωσον σεαυτὸν βιοῦν ὡς τέλειον καὶ προκόπτοντα· καὶ πᾶν τὸ βέλτιστον φαινόμενον ἔστω σοι νόμος ἀπαράβατος. κἂν ἐπίπονόν τι ᾖ ἡδὺ ᾖ ἔνδοξον ἢ ἄδοξον προσάγηται, μέμνησο, ὅτι νῦν ὁ ἀγὼν καὶ ἤδη πάρεστι τὰ Ὀλύμπια καὶ οὐκ ἔστιν ἀναβάλλεσθαι οὐκέτι καὶ ὅτι παρὰ μίαν ἡμέραν καὶ ἓν πρᾶγμα καὶ ἀπόλλυται προκοπὴ καὶ σῴζεται.

Σωκράτης οὕτως ἀπετελέσθη, ἐπὶ πάντων τῶν προσαγομένων αὐτῷ μηδενὶ ἄλλῳ προσέχων ἢ

precepts which you ought to accept, and you have accepted them. Why then do you still wait for a master, that you may delay the amendment of yourself till he comes? You are a youth no longer, you are now a full-grown man. If now you are careless and indolent and are always putting off, fixing one day after another as the limit when you mean to begin attending to yourself, then, living or dying, you will make no progress but will continue unawares in ignorance. Therefore make up your mind before it is too late to live as one who is mature and proficient, and let all that seems best to you be a law that you cannot transgress. And if you encounter anything troublesome or pleasant or glorious or inglorious, remember that the hour of struggle is come, the Olympic contest is here and you may put off no longer, and that one day and one action determines whether the progress you have achieved is lost or maintained.

This was how Socrates attained perfection, paying heed to nothing but reason, in all that he encountered. And if you are not yet Socrates, yet

τῷ λόγῳ. σὺ δὲ εἰ καὶ μήπω εἶ Σωκράτης, ὡς Σωκράτης γε εἶναι βουλόμενος ὀφείλεις βιοῦν.

52

Ὁ πρῶτος καὶ ἀναγκαιότατος τόπος ἐστὶν ἐν φι-
λοσοφίᾳ ὁ τῆς χρήσεως τῶν θεωρημάτων, οἷον
τὸ μὴ ψεύδεσθαι· ὁ δεύτερος ὁ τῶν ἀποδείξεων,
οἷον πόθεν ὅτι οὐ δεῖ ψεύδεσθαι· τρίτος ὁ αὐτῶν
τούτων βεβαιωτικὸς καὶ διαρθρωτικός, οἷον πόθεν ὅτι τοῦτο ἀπόδειξις; τί γάρ ἐστιν ἀπόδειξις, τί
ἀκολουθία, τί μάχη, τί ἀληθές, τί ψεῦδος; οὐκοῦν
ὁ μὲν τρίτος τόπος ἀναγκαῖος διὰ τὸν δεύτερον, ὁ
δὲ δεύτερος διὰ τὸν πρῶτον· ὁ δὲ ἀναγκαιότατος
καὶ ὅπου ἀναπαύεσθαι δεῖ, ὁ πρῶτος. ἡμεῖς δὲ
ἔμπαλιν ποιοῦμεν· ἐν γὰρ τῷ τρίτῳ τόπῳ δια-
τρίβομεν καὶ περὶ ἐκεῖνόν ἐστιν ἡμῖν ἡ πᾶσα
σπουδή· τοῦ δὲ πρώτου παντελῶς ἀμελοῦμεν.
τοιγαροῦν ψευδόμεθα μέν, πῶς δὲ ἀποδείκνυται
ὅτι οὐ δεῖ ψεύδεσθαι, πρόχειρον ἔχομεν.

ought you to live as one who would wish to be a Socrates.

52

The first and most necessary department of philosophy deals with the application of principles; for instance, 'not to lie'. The second deals with demonstrations; for instance, 'How comes it that one ought not to lie?' The third is concerned with establishing and analysing these processes; for instance, 'How comes it that this is a demonstration? What is demonstration, what is consequence, what is contradiction, what is true, what is false?' It follows then that the third department is necessary because of the second, and the second because of the first. The first is the most necessary part, and that in which we must rest. But we reverse the order: we occupy ourselves with the third, and make that our whole concern, and the first we completely neglect. Wherefore we lie, but are ready enough with the demonstration that lying is wrong.

53

Ἐπὶ παντὸς πρόχειρα ἑκτέον ταῦτα·

ἄγου δέ μ᾽, ὦ Ζεῦ, καὶ σύ γ᾽ ἡ Πεπρωμένη,
ὅποι ποθ᾽ ὑμῖν εἰμι διατεταγμένος·
ὡς ἕψομαί γ᾽ ἄοκνος· ἢν δέ γε μὴ θέλω,
κακὸς γενόμενος, οὐδὲν ἧττον ἕψομαι.

«ὅστις δ᾽ ἀνάγκῃ συγκεχώρηκεν καλῶς,
σοφὸς παρ᾽ ἡμῖν, καὶ τὰ θεῖ᾽ ἐπίσταται».

«ἀλλ᾽, ὦ Κρίτων, εἰ ταύτῃ τοῖς θεοῖς φίλον,
ταύτῃ γενέσθω».

«ἐμὲ δὲ Ἄνυτος καὶ Μέλιτος ἀποκτεῖναι μὲν
δύνανται, βλάψαι δὲ οὔ».

53

On every occasion we must have these thoughts
at hand,

'Lead me, O Zeus, and lead me, Destiny,
Whither ordainèd is by your decree.
I'll follow, doubting not, or if with will
Recreant I falter, I shall follow still.'[2]

'Who rightly with necessity complies
In things divine we count him skilled and wise.'[3]

'Well, Crito, if this be the gods' will, so be it.'[4]

'Anytus and Meletus have power to put me
to death, but not to harm me.'[5]

---

2. Cleanthes
3. Euripides, Fragment 965
4. Plato, *Crito*, 43d
5. Plato, *Apology*, 30c

**ALSO FROM
AIORA PRESS:**

Myths Behind Words

GREEK MYTHOLOGY IN ENGLISH WORDS AND EXPRESSIONS

Compiled by Alexander Zaphiriou
Illustrated by Panagiotis Stavropoulos

This collection retells the myths behind common words and expressions in English, bringing to life the heroes, monsters and gods whose deeds and battles have left a hidden mark on our language.

AN ANTHOLOGY

Words of Wisdom from Ancient Greece

BILINGUAL EDITION

Translated by Alexander Zaphiriou
Illustrated by Panagiotis Stavropoulos

Words of Wisdom from Ancient Greece gathers the best of a thousand years of philosophy, history and literature, in a compilation of writing spanning from 800 BCE to 200 CE. This survey of ancient wisdom offers guidance for a life well lived from luminaries of Greece's legendary past.

ARISTOTLE
On Happiness
BILINGUAL EDITION

NICOMACHEAN ETHICS - BOOK X
Translated by H. Rackham

Aristotle contributed to practically all branches of human knowledge; in fact, he is widely regarded as the founder of Western science. In Book X of *Nicomachean Ethics*, included in this volume, the great philosopher discusses what happiness is and how to achieve it.

EPICURUS
In Pursuit of Pleasure
BILINGUAL EDITION

Translated by Cyril Bailey

This volume contains Cyril Bailey's masterly, classic translations of the most important surviving writing of Epicurus and offers the contemporary reader a comprehensive overview of Epicurean Ethics, his philosophy on what matters in life and how we should live.

HIPPOCRATES
Aphorisms
BILINGUAL EDITION

Translated by W.H.S. Jones

Hippocrates of Kos is credited with being the first healer to separate the discipline of medicine from religion, arguing that disease was not a punishment inflicted by the gods but rather the product of environmental factors, diet and lifestyle.

196